Int|AR

Interventions | **Adaptive Reuse**

Editors In Chief:
Markus Berger
Liliane Wong

Special Editor:
Jeffrey Katz

Graphic Design Editor:
Ernesto Aparicio

Int|AR is an annual publication by the editors in chief: Markus Berger + Liliane Wong, and the Department of Interior Architecture, Rhode Island School of Design.

Members of the Advisory Board:
- Heinrich Hermann, Professor of Architecture, SUNY College of Technology, Alfred State; Head of the Advisory Board, Co-Founder of Int|AR
- Uta Hassler, Chair of Historic Building Research and Conservation, ETH Zurich.
- Brian Kernaghan, Professor Emeritus of Interior Architecture, RISD.
- Niklaus Kohler, Professor Emeritus, Karlsruhe Institute of Technology.
- Dietrich Neumann, Royce Family Professor for the History of Modern Architecture and Urban Studies at Brown University.
- Theodore H M Prudon, Professor of Historic Preservation, Columbia University; President of Docomomo USA.
- August Sarnitz, Professor of History of Architecture, Academy of Fine Arts Vienna.
- Friedrich St Florian, FAIA, Professor Emeritus of Architecture, RISD; Principal, Friedrich St. Florian Architects, Providence, RI.
- Wilfried Wang, O'Neil Ford Centennial Professor in Architecture, University of Texas, Austin; Hoidn Wang Partner, Berlin.

Layout_Marianna Bender, Jin Hee Kim

Editorial & Communications Assistant_Lea Hershkowitz

Design Coordination_Marianna Bender

Cover Design_Ernesto Aparicio, Marianna Bender

Cover Photo_Courtesy of Comme des Garçons

Inner Cover Photos_Alaina Bernstein, Nick Heywood

Support Team_Pamela Harrington, Jisoo Kim, Ben Shuai, Liming Jiang, Clara Halston

Printed by SYL, Barcelona

Distributed by Birkauser Verlag GmbH, Basel P.O. Box 44, 4009 Basel, Switzerland, Part of Walter de Gruyter GmbH, Berlin/Boston

Int|AR welcomes responses to articles in this issue and submissions of essays or projects for publication in future issues. All submitted materials are subject to editorial review. Please address feedback, inquiries, and other materials to the Editors, **Int|AR Journal**, **Department of Interior Architecture**, **Rhode Island School of Design**, Two College Street Providence, RI 02903 www.intar-journal.edu, email: INTARjournal@risd.edu

CONTENTS

AN INVENTORY OF EXPERIENCE

by LILIANE WONG

On my first sabbatical, I photographed the graffiti covered walls of a 19th century brick slaughterhouse turned shelter for the homeless in a fringe area of Rome. In 2014, I returned on a subsequent sabbatical to discover it transformed into MACRO Testaccio, a part of Rome's museums of contemporary art, the graffiti a remnant of my memory. This once forsaken wedge of land by the Tiber inhabited by an abandoned abattoir and a defunct gasometer had been claimed as a new venue of experience for the artistic avant-garde, searching for new grounds. Between two sabbaticals, the *experience economy* happened.

The transformation of a slaughterhouse in a former industrial neighborhood of Rome to a vibrant art venue was part of an urban renewal of the Ostiense Marconi area. The conversion of this industrial zone to a cultural hub exemplifies an embrace of the industrial past, as seen at similar conversions such as the Zollverein Coal Mine Industrial Complex or Mass MoCA. In Rome, this is most evident in the conversion of the Montemartini Thermoelectric Centre for housing the Musei Capitolini's collection of classical sculpture within the defunct machines of electric production. The role played by the existing structures of industry for the production of new experience is an example of Pine and Gilmore's experience economy applied to the practice of adaptive reuse. Since the introduction of this principle in a 1998 *Harvard Business Review* article, we have witnessed the transformation of experience into a commodity.

Experience is defined as "the act or process of directly perceiving events or reality." As a commodity, experience has expanded in scope. The merchandising of experience is a business, leaving no economic tier untouched. From travel to food, it addresses the desires of a society consumed with consumption. In the experience economy, scaling Mt. Everest is not only the glory attained by years of training but also a travel adventure purchased through the backs of sherpas who shoulder packs, oxygen and sometimes even the climbers themselves. In the experience economy, indulging in sweets takes on new significance for the weight conscious with Harvard professor David Edward's *Le Whif*, an inhaled aerosol that provides the experience of chocolate without the calories. In tangible and intangible form the consumption of experience has proliferated and assimilated into our daily existence.

Today's technologies have furthered redefined the definition of experience with a new found temporality. The means to "perceive directly" has changed dramatically with virtual and augmented reality. Being there and taking part of things are now interpreted on a different clock in which our physical presence has little bearing. With a host of possibilities from tweets to the voyeurism enabled by photo messaging apps everyone is always *in* on the experience.

What is experience?

Our understanding today of the adventures of the Trojan War of the 12th to 13th centuries B.C. is derived from centuries of the retelling of the epic narration attributed to the mysterious bard, Homer. Purported to have been born between the 12th and 8th centuries B.C. our experience of the launching of the thousand ships is only through his words.

What of the sensory experience evoked by the famed madeleine in Proust's *Remembrance of Things Past*? Are aerosol truffles any less delectable? Can we equally hear the bantering between the sonorous 'Knight of the Doleful Countenance' and the practical Sancho Panza in the words of Cervantes' *Don Quixote* as in the deep resonance of the cello and the quick notes of the viola in Richard Strauss' symphonic poem of the same name?

When is experience authentic?

The dioramas of Ai Weiwei from his six-part work, *S.A.C.R.E.D.*, document his 81 days of imprisonment and place us directly and with photographic clarity in his jail cell. Telehealth provides a different experience

LEFT
Homeless shelter in the Testaccio neighborhood
Rome, 2009

RIGHT
***"The Machines and the Gods,"* Centrale Montemartini**
Museum, Rome

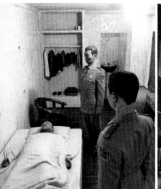   

in healthcare in which a visit to the doctor takes place through telecommunication technologies. An American news anchor mistakenly conflates experiences in a helicopter, claiming one that never took place.

Within the built environment, William Morris' Society for the Protection of Ancient Buildings articulated a stance on "restoration" that offered the repair of old buildings as an alternative where such skill lay "in mending them with the minimum loss of fabric and ...... authenticity. Old buildings cannot be preserved by making them new."[1]

What is [that] authenticity?

In "The Weather Project," Olafur Eliasson's creation of the sun in the Turbine Room of the Tate Modern Museum, the mechanics of his installation are purposefully exposed. With an interest in the way "information influences experience," he provides an experience of the artificial sun that addresses the "discrepancy between the experience of seeing and the knowledge or expectation of what we are seeing."[2]

Our authors in Volume 06 grapple with these fascinating and complex issues of experience, both in and out of the economy. We are offered insight into the application of the principles of Pine and Gilmore in the reuse of the built environment: guerrilla retail, restaurants, hotels, museums, expositions and other "cathedrals of commerce." Pine and Gilmore also inspired speculations beyond the tangible to other realms of reality: virtual, augmented and even denied. In Volume 06, we also offer for the first time a combined interview and photo-essay on the work of the Madrid firm, Nieto Sobejano Arquitectos. From their project for San Telmo Museum in San Sebastián, the European Capital of Culture 2016, we follow their work of adaptation and revision as "an invention of memory."

"[M]emory calls up lived experience, it is precise, exact, implacable, but it produces nothing new; that is its limitation. The imagination, however, cannot call up

anything, because it cannot remember, and that is its limitation but by way of compensation it produces the new, something that wasn't there before, that has never been there."[3]

Euclid's Fifth Postulate states that, "[i]f two lines are drawn which intersect a third in such a way that the sum of the inner angles on one side is less than two right angles, then the two lines inevitably must intersect each other on that side if extended far enough." Today we reduce this principle to two parallel lines never meet. In a curved, non-Euclidean space, parallel is defined instead by the negation of Euclid's Fifth, "[i]f l is any line and P is any point not on l, then there are no lines through P that are parallel to l." An experience we may never encounter in our Euclidean existence may be one that we cannot avoid in non-Euclidean space.

In the Rain Room at MoMA PS1, a visitor negotiates a torrential rain that ceases to fall only where he steps. In the Bay of Biscay, while installing his monumental steel structures, *Comb of the Wind,* sculptor Eduardo Chillida negotiates sprays of water lapping at the temporary scaffolding in the sea. Almost five decades apart, these encounters with water demonstrate an evolving continuum of experience.

"Why is experience oriented towards knowledge and perception towards knowing?"[4]

Providence, March 2015

ENDNOTES

1 "SPAB's Purpose," http://www.spab.org.uk

2 "Olafur Eliasson: The Weather Project," http://www.tate.org.uk

3 Tabucchi, Antonio. (translated by Alistair McEwan) *It's Getting Later All the Time*, New Directions Books, Antonella Antonelli Letteria SRI, Milan, 2001, p 139.

4 Chillida, Eduardo. (translated by Luis Sacristán Murga),"Speech in the Doctorate Honoris Causa Ceremony," University of Alicante, 1996.

FAR LEFT
S.A.C.R.E.D., Venice, Ai Weiwei

CENTER LEFT
The Weather Project, Olafur Eliasson

CENTER RIGHT
The Rain Room, Random International

FAR RIGHT
Comb of the Wind in construction, Eduardo Chillida

Main Hall of taxidermy at Cairo Agriculture Museum

NEW PASTS, OLD EXPERIENCES

THE SPECTACLE OF AUTHENTICITY
AT CAIRO'S MUSEUM OF AGRICULTURE

by SAMAA ELIMAM

Set within an urban retreat of botanical gardens at the heart of a busy Cairo neighborhood is a cabinet of curiosities with high ceilings and concealed rooms, structures that seem paused in time and nearly untouched since their inauguration. Camel organs, preserved disease worms, and a buffalo milking apparatus are displayed side by side in cases against the backdrop of a mid-19th century palace. Galleries are organized according to subtopics, often straying towards disease and nutrition, artisanal crafts, and natural history. Column arcades adorned with intricate cornices are lined with wood cabinets of bird species and overlook double-height spaces that frame folk dancing mannequins, all washed with sunlight from the clerestories above. Wooden wall panels mounted with python skin, a lion's head, and hunting spears embrace a grand marble staircase streaming light from high French windows. The top floor is centered on a large elliptical atrium; showpieces include horse, camel, and whale skeletons, with giraffe and gazelle heads distributed throughout endless arched openings. Original drawings of the 1964 UNESCO project to rescue Abu Simbel, a diorama of the Aswan High Dam and its electricity revenues, solid wood models of the Delta and its 1930s agricultural outputs, and stained glass windows depicting the daily lives of fellahin, all address critical moments and idiosyncrasies in Egypt's history. An atmosphere comparable only to a film set, the nearly 80 year old Agriculture Museum in Cairo serves as a fantastical spatial timeline through the nation's imaginary imagery at multiple scales, both obvious and obscure.

Urban explorers searching for an unexpected narrative have recently rediscovered the museum, indicating interest in a history other than what is now considered mainstream tourism in Egypt. Conceptualizing the renewed interest in this urban pocket within its current context reveals the rise of a new economy that yearns for authenticity, and reveres fantastical experiences. Clear parallels can be drawn between the contemporary consumption of experience and late 19th century Romanticism that drove the fascination with ancient ruins and led to the founding of the archaeological field. Every age seeks new pasts mediated through historical buildings, ruins, and artifacts, converging to construct unparalleled settings. Though in reality they have always existed, these places and objects regain a central presence in the cultural sphere, reanimated as if becoming only just unearthed.

Architecture as a discipline has recently witnessed a resurgent trend in the consumption of cultural experiences: the rediscovery of abandoned buildings, decayed industrial sites, and disaster ruins reflects a preoccupation with the uncovering of alternative subcultures. Understanding the experience economy at the turn-of-the-century vis à vis the contemporary phenomenon reveals that, beyond merely the pursuit of authenticity, it is the expectation of the authentic that drives the desire for immersion within that which evokes the rare and genuine. Though, as Theodor Adorno argues, authenticity and its aura is not so much a critique of modernity as it is a "waste product of the modern that it attacks."[1] Preservation practices, including the renovation, expansion, maintenance, and restoration of cultural buildings, coincide with critical moments of development and modernization efforts.[2] The introduction of these efforts questions and unsettles socially accepted and culturally established images of history, giving rise to a phenomenological conception of the past that requires substantiation through original, physical evidence. With every declaration to modernize, the past takes on a renewed relevance that conjures up redefinitions of social and cultural values. At the core of this process are issues of authenticity and preservation – what is real, what to protect, what to destroy, and what to market – as a platform upon which modernity can thrive. In the case of Egypt, this manifests itself across all of its historical eras: previously in its ancient history, then its Islamic

Late 1880s British tourists visiting the Great Pyramids and Sphinx

heritage and, later, in a heightened rural and agricultural past. Currently recovering from another crisis of national identity, the delineation of a simple and innocent past quells the obstacles to transition within society's perception.

Looking In, Looking Out

The recent rediscovery of this museum has an interesting parallel with Egypt's socio-economic and political history since the 1930s. Europe was immersed in the repercussions of Egyptomania, a fascination with ancient Egypt first triggered by Napoleon's 1798 campaign. Amid the allure of ancient ruins and archaeology during the late 19th century, European tourists were themselves traveling on expeditions to Egypt, complete with the experience of riding a camel or donkey around the Pyramids of Giza. The British travel agency Thomas Cook & Son regularly took tour groups to Egypt in the 1880s, but it was not until 1920 that they had established offices throughout its cities including Cairo, Luxor, Aswan, and Alexandria.[3] At the height of European tourism to Egypt, Cook & Son had created the Nile Voyage package that took travelers on a cruise down the river aboard luxury steamboats. Made further idyllic through the transportation artery that created Egyptian civilization itself, the experience of sailing along the pure Nile landscape further accentuated this romanticism. Continuing with discoveries of Nefertiti's bust in 1912 and Tutankhamun's tomb in 1922, the obsession drove a new mode of tourist consumption that relied on fortuitous experiences and encounters. Egypt's antiquarian past sparked an endless mystery and exoticism in the European imagination that lingered within its enduring ruins and monuments.

At home, Egypt's cultural self-recognition experienced a turbulent transformation. The 1930s was a decade of disillusionment in Egyptian society, wrought between Eastern and Western principles and fragmented ideologies that caused cultural and intellectual confusion.[4] Led by the Wafd Party, the Egyptian Revolution of 1919 against the British occupation promised self-determination and sovereignty, but led instead to nominal independence and weakened social and political institutions. As the representation of the people, the Wafd was becoming increasingly ineffective in the face of the Palace and the British. Further, the Great Depression resulted in a drastic decrease in the world value of cotton, one of Egypt's most reliable exports, leaving the country in search of alternative economic options.[5]

The decade witnessed a dramatic shift in Egypt's social geography. The decline in cotton profit brought rapid urbanization, as migrants searched for employment opportunities in the city. Further, educational growth, particularly the number of youth receiving higher learning, noticeably increased, producing a consumer generation with a modern, educated background. The growing student population had a direct role in redefin-

Main Hall of taxidermy at Cairo Agriculture Museum

ing the country's national identity and, thus, its cultural production.[6] The result was the gradual estrangement from the country's rural origins, mobilizing them as the base for an oncoming, newly-established modernity. In this sense, the processes and practices of laying claim to authenticity was in and of itself a mode of cultural production.[7] For many, the shift to the city brought with it an inadvertent image of the nation putting aside its agrarian roots. Although the majority of the country's population was still rural, the escalating centralization of Cairo attempted to lay out a landscape of cultural institutions made for urban consumption. These institutions could not deny that the rural played a critical role in the country's history and development, but one that could now be archived as a phase in its past.

Regal Grounds
On the ground, greater urbanization required increased accessibility throughout the Delta, prompting a series of large-scale infrastructure projects. The Palace developed a new department of transportation that paved

and set roads, rail, and water routes, as well as a new communication and postal sector. To increase awareness of modernization efforts, new cultural institutions accompanied and took record of these developments. The Egyptian Railroad Museum was built for the International Railway Conference in 1933, and the Egyptian Postal Museum started as a royal stamp collection in 1934, growing to an extended record of postal communication in 1940.[8] Yet of these initiatives, the Museum of Agriculture's topics of interest, obscure collections, and, most particularly, its reuse of royal buildings, provoke questions of projected authenticity that have recurred time and again, from the turn-of-the-century to current rediscovery. The idea for the Museum was advocated by King Fuad in 1929, and inaugurated in 1938 by his son, King Farouk. Originally the grounds of the two palaces of Princess Fatima Ismail, King Fuad's sister and the daughter of Khedive Ismail, the land is comprised of 125,000 square meters which the Princess had dedicated to the development of Cairo University.[9] The land was transferred to the Ministry of Agriculture once the

Preserved animal organs organized in wooden cabinets

University built its own premises, and the Museum opened to the public in 1938 as the world's first agriculture collection.[10] Remaining dormant from 1952 until 1987, its 1996 restoration and expansion, as well as its overly extravagant curatorial content, have driven its reemergence and circulation through digital media.[11] The Museum of Agriculture's adaptive reuse stands witness to the misalignments and contradictions that triggered its founding, and still exist to this day.

Spectacle of Authenticity

At first impression, the Museum assembles its overarching agricultural theme as a way to reflect on the social and cultural geography of particular phases in the country's history. Yet the setting captures much more than this: it is a promenade through the oscillations of Egypt's cultural identity, from the turbulence of its colonial past, through its Ottoman monarchy, the instabilities of a mid-century revolution, remnants of its pan-Arab associations and chapters through its modern presidents and their hefty public works projects. In addition to their collections, the buildings construct a narrative that attests to how Egypt's cultural and political trials are inseparable from its natural and environmental past. The overlay of rural and royal, such as juxtapositions of clay pottery alongside khedival silk carpets, illustrate the layered histories and intricate narratives that compose the country. Tiers of self-projected romanticism are revealed through the spectacles of the Museum. The attempt at the production of an authentic atmosphere is overstated, leaving the visitor with the image of multiple, superimposed conceptions of the rural as the other. The modern visitor gazes at a 1930s spectacle depicting images of the countryside, ironically still regular scenes and practices to this day. The spectator is positioned within the cycle of projected authenticity, exuding an unmistakably post-colonial aura, that is decidedly inauthentic.

Apart from mandatory school field trips, the Museum is gaining ground with independent travelers as well as tour groups. Spread through personal travel blogs, websites for unique places, and online travel agencies, the Museum is becoming reanimated at a time when the country is yet again experiencing a resurgence of history and culture into its collective memory. Along with these rediscovered venues, boutique hotels and services catering to a counter-culture are surfacing alongside conventional models of tourism that have existed since Cook & Son. Besides its ancient monuments and colorful bazaars, visitors and locals alike are becoming interested in embedded narratives within a complex and layered history.

As for self-awareness, the country is recognizing that an imposed expectation of authenticity is an inevitable and recurring theme in its history. Here, Adorno's argument holds true: presenting a simple past that relies on roots and origins, as a rarity to be exhibited and consumed, is a renewed product of modernization.[12] In this sense, pausing the past is necessary in order to look forward to a more progressive future. In common is the selection of history particular to each era, and the constant expectation to deliver authenticity upon which modernity can thrive. Made for urban cultural consumption, the experience of the Museum is a simulation of the rural that paradoxically characterizes most of the country just outside of its major urban centers. The Princess' palace-turned-agricultural spectacle inserts itself into the urban memory, embodying the reality of layered, often contradictory histories. After a period of tumultuous events in 2011 and 2013, society is facing yet again another phase of economic and political reshuffling, including the initiation of new public works projects at the Suez Canal. The disruption in the rhythm of daily life and the necessity of institutional reordering instigates a renewed hold on the past. Borrowing from and expanding on post-colonial projections, the Museum mobilizes the spectacle of authenticity – and society's quest for it – to ground itself as a tangible, cultural anchor within the country's collective consciousness.

ENDNOTES

1 Adorno, Theodor W. *The Language of Authenticity*, translated by Knut Tarnowski and Frederic Will (Evanston: Northwestern University Press, 1973), 45.

2 Koolhaas, Rem. "Preservation is Overtaking Us," *Future Anterior*, Vol.1, No. 2, Fall 2004.

3 Coleman, Anthony. *Millenium,* (Transworld Publishers, 1999), 231-233.

4 Gershoni, Israel and James P. Jankowski, *Redefining the Egyptian Nation, 1930-1945* (Cambridge: Cambridge University Press, 1995), 3.

5 Gershoni and Jankowski, 6.

6 Gershoni and Jankowski, 3.

7 Adorno, 45.

8 Samih, Mai. "The Grassroots on Display," *Al-Ahram Weekly,* Issue No. 1129, January 3, 2013 (accessed September 23, 2014).

9 Samih, "The Grassroots on Display."

10 Hassan, Fayza. "The Forgotten Museums of Egypt," *Museum: Heritage Landscape of Egypt,* No. 225-226, Vol LVII, 2005 (accessed September 23, 2014), 47.

11 Hassan, 47.

12 Adorno, 45.

APPROXIMATIONS TO A WORKING SPACE

AROUND BUT NOT INSIDE EL MUSEO DE LOS SURES

by LAURA F. GIBELLINI

"Invention always belongs to a man as the inventing subject. [...] Man himself, the human world, is defined by the human subject's aptitude for invention, in the double sense of narrative fiction or historical fabulation and of technical or technoepistemic innovation." Jacques Derrida, Psyche: Inventions of the Other.[1]

This paper is the manifestation of an unfulfilled quest, and an exploration of the conditions that favor the existence of a certain space. It is first and foremost an attempt to delineate the conditions that allow life to happen: An attempt to tap into the elements that define the specificity of a given location and how one can think of the economy of experience when the 'actual' experience and accessibility (to such space or built environment) is denied.

Considered as a work in progress, where images should be read together with the text, *Approximations* is an invention, an experiment that might very well fail in its attempt to ascribe a certain sense to a removed object of study. It may, nonetheless, serve as a meditation on the fluid condition of human existence, and the constructed nature of experience itself.

The Beginning

This project began with an invitation by *El Museo de los Sures,*[2] in South Williamsburg, to be an artist in residence over the late summer of 2014. I had planned, with this residency, to create a think-tank through which to explore the relation of various components of my own practice to the built environment (the neighborhood) and its people (residents and visitors) and to transcribe my reflections for the present volume of *Int|AR*. However due to a scheduling issue, I am unable get into the space and have a first-hand experience of its specificity. Yet, as I have grown more and more interested in exploring the fundamental conditions that allow life to happen, and how such conditions could be represented, I decided to develop my practice *around* the space itself—and to reflect on the experience of the endless approximation to its fundamental means of existence.

Reflecting on this difficulty of representing conditions that allow life, and my inability to access the space itself (and related issues of impossibility, accessibility and even failure) also became fundamental. The following are my findings.

ON THE CONDITIONS THAT ALLOW LIFE TO HAPPEN

An Introduction

According to recent research[3] on the origin of life and its subsequent evolution, it may very well be possible that under certain conditions (in this case, a thermal bath similar to the atmosphere or the ocean, driven by an external source of energy such as the sun, according to Doctor Jeremy England the leading scientist behind this experiment's potential breakthrough) matter would

acquire the fundamental physical attributes associated with life. Based on established formulas derived from the second law of thermodynamics, scientists may be closer to finding a broader perspective on the emergence of living organisms beyond Darwinian explanations. Central to this research is the notion of self-replication and entropy, and how "potential fitness is set by how effectively it [a self-replicator] exploits sources of energy in its environment to catalyze its own reproduction."[4]

While self-replication or spontaneous generation is beyond the scope of this article, its focus on how the conditions of a specific environment determine life, even at the very first moment of its creation, seems both relevant and crucial. The hollow cliché of environment affecting life, taken more literally, carries greater meaning and continues to elude a clear determination of precisely why and how life began, the conditions that allowed it to happen in the first place.[5]

Like the thermal bath described above, the two principal elements guiding this project are the atmospheric conditions of the site and its oceanic nature, a self-contained but fluid and fluctuating environment.

On Atmospheric Conditions

When Peter Sloterdijk reflects on Heidegger's notion of *being-in-the-world* (Dasein) or being *thrown* into the world, he concludes that it means being inside some form of sphere, some atmo-sphere.[6] Indeed, in his trilogy *Spheres,* Sloterdijk argues how the creation of different forms of spherical entities (bubbles, globes) and compounds (foams)—considered as immunized self-contained unities designed to self-replicate and subsist in foreign territories—defines human existence, its organization (plurality) and its expansion (globalization). His is a spatial approach to western metaphysics, from the womb to the Greek polis to the small urban apartment to globalization...

According to Sloterdijk, air-conditioning—the possibility of creating a controlled environment where the *air* becomes explicit, something that can be altered and reconfigured—has become a fundamental part of a system that makes our life possible.[7] In his view then, air-conditioning and atmospheric conditions mark and define life, a life contained by more or less porous walls.

Consider the glass house, which is fundamental to Sloterdijk's thinking.[8] It is a construction, a built environment wherein climatic conditions are replicated in order for certain plants and organisms to flourish as they would in their natural habitat. It is a technological process that allows life to subsist in a foreign environment. Analogous to the glass house are other spaces and territories, contained by built walls or geopolitical boundaries. One can also reflect on different forms of territorialization and naturalization that are similarly implemented—except that with a human being, the original displacement and fragility of this life-support system becomes even more apparent (and precarious). As Sloterdijk argues, the Greek polis itself—and the basis of democratic societies as we know them—is an artificial construct that solved the problem of bringing strangers together to coexist behind shared walls and a naturalized climate. It allowed, through the rule of *nomos* (law) and the implementation of rituals that strengthened the citizen's sense of commonality, the creation of a public sphere. With these, a shared community appeared, one determined by very specific normative conditions that served to prevent individual actors from manifesting particularized agency.

On an Oceanic Nature

When thinking about habitats, places, environments, envelopes, and bubbles one has to acknowledge their porous nature, their fluidity. Atmospheres and bubbles subsist in a certain liquid state and are permeable and in flux. They are surrounded by membranes rather than by thick insurmountable walls. Similarly, we observe the fluid and liquid nature of our own sociopolitical environment. The solid structures and rigidity that marked both pre-modern and modern eras have weakened, no longer serving as frames of reference for human actions as rigidly as they once did; long-term life plans do not seem as feasible anymore, the fundamental pillars that sustained our ordered world melting before us (namely the family, class and neighborhood as Ulrich Beck would point out); our existence is increasingly more fragile, uncertain and fragmented, the exercise of power itself overcoming political boundaries and emerging as extraterritorial. Yet rather than analyzing the socio-political consequences of this *liquid modernity*[9] I'd like to focus, more literally, on the *aquatic* nature of the specific site that we are contemplating.

El Museo de los Sures is located in South Williamsburg, Brooklyn. Walking west from *El Museo*, the street ends with a wall that seems to obliterate the aquatic condition of the location, negating its fluid nature. But as ones turns the next corner the urban landscape opens up to the East River—in actuality not a river but a salt-water tidal strait that separates Long Island from Manhattan, also an island, and from the North American mainland.

At the mercy of the tides, the water flow of the East River changes direction frequently, in tune with the (North) Atlantic Ocean. As the sea level rises, and the Atlantic responds to the world's changing conditions, so does the risk of flooding. I am interested in this source of instability and what such aqueous nature might tells us.

Oceanic representations take their form from representations of land. Like those maps, ocean is represented through a series of latitude-longitude points characterized by constant values across key variables[10] —effectively obliterating both the mutable surface of the water and its fluid dynamic that unfolds across time and space. This exposes the fundamental limitations of transposing terrestrial forms of representation onto oceanic ones. Points in the water are aqueous, not terrestrial, and their mobility implies dispersion and the impossibility of territorialization. The ocean allows movement but it is also constituted by and constitutive of movement. It produces difference even if it serves as a unifying medium.

If we consider movement *as* geography[11] and how geophysical mobility is the nature of land and aqueous masses, then we can conceive of space less as a stationary framework. Rather we can re-conceptualize it as a medium that is constantly being remade. Fluid dynamics might suggest, as Steinberg[12] notes, a route to developing decentered ontologies of connection. The ocean, more than merely a series of terrestrial points linked by connections, is a space of connections itself, where its underlying liquid nature appears as the context for human activities. As described above, these are more and more fluid, dynamic and unstable—without reference to any fixed grid of places or coordinates.

And yet the ocean also remains a mystery as it offers only a partial encounter, almost immediately substituted by a succession of others. An endless approximation and the abandonment of the possibility of a fixed nature remain its only plausible approach and means of comprehension.

The gaps in oceanic representations, as well as the gaps in atmospheric depictions, testify to how that which remains unrepresentable becomes unacknowledged, and how the unacknowledged becomes unthinkable.[13] It is this which is unthinkable that interests me, the gap, that which remains hidden and we are constantly looking for, even without knowing what it is.

For this reason, this project involves the endless approximation introduced at the beginning—as working *around* the subject matter itself. Working on the edges emerges as the only plausible means of comprehension. After all, only partial encounters seem now possible.

An Endless Approximation

With the above in mind, several questions arise: How can one think about the specificity of air, of atmospheric conditions, and of the oceanic nature of a given site? How can one render such intangible conditions visible? And how might such conditions affect the different forms of existence that strive to flourish in that place? Finally, how can one draw a meaningful and in some way defined experience from such research?

The images on this paper offer an approach to these issues, as they depict different, perhaps more indirect engagement with the (urban) landscape. They are an attempt to register the impermanence of the fleeting nature of experience through the practice of, literally, drawn attempts and approximations. It is the search of understanding through the making, the

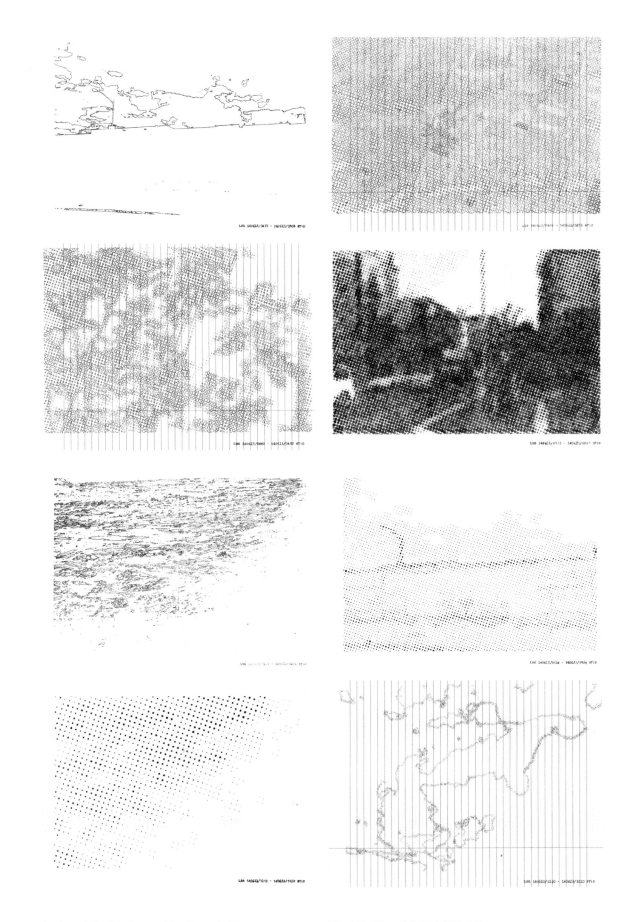

Landscape 3: South 1st Street and Kent Avenue, 11249.
Tree 1: 120 South 1st Street, 11249. 26.07.2014-11.08.2014
Landscape 1: East River. 26.07.2014-11.08.2014
Landscape 2: East River. 26.07.2014-12.08.2014

Wave 1: East River. 26.07.2014-11.08.2014
Landscape 6: South 1st Street and Bedford Avenue, 11249.
25.07.2014-20.08.2014
Landscape 4: South 1st Street and Kent Avenue, 11249.
25.07.2014-15.08.2014
Cloud 1: South 1st Street, 11249. 26.07.2014-11.08.2014

intangible knowledge that emerges in the practice that I am calling for.

Focusing on the representation of the most tangible parts of the atmosphere and ocean—clouds and waves—and on key locations around *El Museo,* these drawings are delineated and composed of clusters of bubbles that are determined by algorithmic interpretations of specific images of the site. The drawings are based on technologies and mechanisms used to monitor changes in the weather and to track the conditions of the air and water—their pollution, temperature, level of humidity, wind and variability. All images are carefully annotated with a description of their atmospheric coordinates and accompanied by a caption that determines the location and the date of capture and its subsequent rendering. The images appear then as mutable charts that aim to fix a transition, an endless in-motion condition, a fluid existence. The inherent impossibility of fixing such a specific image, and the endlessness of the approximation, become apparent here as the fundamental experience of the site.

As an Epilogue

Mine is a first and holistic approach to the nature of South Williamsburg that avoids relating directly to its built environment due to the denial of access to a specific space. Pushed to the edges, the consideration of the mutable nature of the atmosphere and the oceans appeared as a fundamental frame of mind from which to consider how the production of 'new' forms of experience are based on repeatable conditions that are nonetheless marked by fluid dynamics that we can, perhaps, try to track and predict in an endless effort, one that nevertheless always contains a gap and an inherent unattainablility—one which defines life itself.

Pertinent questions might be how and why Williamsburg is changing and what types of experiences are urban planners and other policy makers fostering in such a setting. What kind of people are populating the neighborhood now and how is it different from earlier communities? And what does this tell us about New York City and the experience of the built environment? How specific can South Williamsburg remain as a product of the real estate market and of mutable fads marked by gentrification tendencies?

These seem particularly urgent and relevant. Yet perhaps it is still a good idea to step back and note how air-conditioned, oceanic, and fluid, our forms of existence are, regardless, even, of the places they occupy.

ENDNOTES

1 Derrida, Jacques. *Psyche: Inventions of the Other*, vol. 1. (California: Standford University Press, 2007), 24 - 25.
2 El Museo de los Sures was created by Southside United HDFC (a community-based, non-profit organization that has undertaken large-scale rehabilitation of many buildings in South Williamsburg) to preserve the history of the neighborhood's residents as the area undergoes gentrification. They now invite artists to develop projects that engage the community and the new experiences that the urban development of the neighborhood entails.
3 England, Jeremy L. "Statistical physics of self-replication", *AIP The Journal of Chemical Physics* 139, 121923 (2013): 1 - 8, accessed August 10, 2014, doi: 10.1063/1.4818538. England is an assistant professor of Physics at the Massachusetts Institute of Technology.
4 Ibid., 3.
5 And it is yet to be proved if this approach is sustainable.
6 Latour, Bruno. "Air" in *Sensorium: Embodied Experience, Technology and Contemporary Art*, ed. Caroline A. Jones (Cambridge, MA: MIT Press, 2006), 107. *Atmen* means to breathe in German.
7 Sloterdijk, Peter. *Sphären III*. Schäume (Frankfurt:

Suhrkamp, 2004).
8 See for example, Peter Sloterdijk, "Atmospheric Politics" in *Making Things Public. Atmospheres of Democracy*, ed. Bruno Latour and Peter Weibel (Cambridge, MA: MIT Press, 2005) 944 - 951.
9 Bauman, Zygmunt. *Liquid Modernity* (Cambridge, UK; Malden, MA: Polity Press, 2000).
10 For a reflection on the mechanisms used in terrestrial maps to represent a given reality see Laura F. Gibellini, "Weltkarten. Panorama", in *Critical Cartography of Art and Visuality in the Global Age*, ed. Ana Maria Guasch and Nasheli Jiménez del Val, (Cambridge: Cambridge Scholars Publishing, 2014), 119-132.
11 Which is the basis of Lagrangian modeling techniques to chart the ocean, where spaces are no longer considered as a stable background but as part of an unfolding through which objects come into being. See Philip E. Steinberg, "Of other seas: metaphors and materialities in maritime regions", *Atlantic Studies*, 10:2, (2013): 160, accessed July 27, 2014, doi: 10.1080/14788810.2013.785192
12 Ibid., 156 - 169.
13 Ibid., 157.

Diner en blanc, Paris

A VISUAL HISTORY OF DINING

A TIMELINE

by ELI FELDMAN

If the basic function of a restaurant is to provide sustenance, its higher calling is to create social and cultural experiences. A dining experience is not only the result of the quality of the food and drink, it is choreographed by a cadre of workers—chefs, wait staff, dishwashers, hostesses, wine directors—and by the space itself.

In The Experience Economy, an article published in The Harvard Business Review in 1998, B. Joseph Pine II and James H. Gilmore note that the most successful companies need four things in order to create an experience for their customers: active participation, passive participation, immersion, and absorption. Restaurants easily hit all of these areas, and the most successful ones understand that the best guest experiences are by design.

One of the things that make restaurants an interesting demonstration of the experience economy is that the other "stages of economic value" that came before have also shaped the restaurant industry; without the industrial economy and the service economy, the idea of a restaurant as we know it would exist in a very different capacity.

This time line is my effort to understand how the subtle and era-defining disruptions in society, economy, and technology shaped the experience of dining and working in restaurants.

1450
THE GUTENBERG PRINTING PRESS

The printing press is introduced making it possible to print books en masse. This massive democratization of information helped to fuel the Enlightenment.

1784
MARIE-ANTONIN CARÊME IS BORN

Carême was one the first chefs to explore the "high art" of French cuisine, effectively giving birth to *haute cuisine* and setting the stage for chefs like Escoffier who would modernize the cuisine after him.

1789
THE FRENCH REVOLUTION AND THE FALL OF BASTILLE

The symbol of French despotism, the Bastille, falls in an uprising and Louis XVI loses power. The aristocrats are displaced and so are their cooks, meaning they have to find a new way to make a living, so they begin creating menus and cooking for restaurants.

1827
DELMONICO IN NYC OPENS

The Delmonico brothers open up the United States' first fine dining restaurant, complete with private dining rooms, in Manhattan.

1860
PULLMAN DINING CAR

Fine dining and the ability to travel the country in a leisurely manner intersect when the Pullman Dining Car begins serving passengers. What could you find on a menu in 1866? Chicken salad, strawberries and cream and white and red wine.

1898
ESCOFFIER AND RITZ TEAM UP IN PARIS

Auguste Escoffier, a chef who had gained a following in France and beyond for updating traditional French cuisine, teams up with Cesar Ritz to open Hôtel Ritz in Paris. Ritz, the namesake and father of the Ritz Carlton chain, worked the front of the house as the maitre d' while Escoffier ran the kitchen according to the "kitchen brigade system." This team created the model for all fine dining restaurants to follow, with clearly defined roles for front and back of the house.

1698

THE ANGEL COFFEEHOUSE IN OXFORD OPENS

The spice trade brought coffee to England and the British began opening up coffee houses aka "penny university" where patrons could convene over coffee instead of beer. Coffeehouses were a staple of the Enlightenment as the best minds of the time could gather and share ideas. Coffeehouses served as the precursor to modern restaurants.

1766
MATHURIN ROZE OPENS UP "RESTAURANT" IN FRANCE

This is the first occurrence of an establishment being called a restaurant.

1765
THE FIRST USE OF THE WORD "RESTAURANT"

"Restaurant" was originally used to describe a restorative broth. 1765 is the first account of it being used.

1903
THE WRIGHT BROTHERS

The Wright brothers' powered glider takes its first flight and covers 120 feet in 12 seconds. This is quite possibly the most disruptive moment in food history because it led to innovation in travel for people and products.

1908
FORD MOTOR COMPANY INTRODUCES THE MODEL T

The car as we know it is introduced to the American public. An upgrade from the horse and buggy, the T was affordable and offered its passengers the opportunity to travel at their leisure. With this mobility, Americans could access a larger area of dining experience.

1924
FERNAND POINT OPENS LA PYRAMIDE

Point, a French chef who believed that he did not have to strictly follow French technique, opens La Pyramide in France and makes it a point to leave the dining room and interact with guests. He is the first celebrity chef.

1919

FIRST COMMERCIAL PASSENGER PLANE BUILT

WWI fueled massive innovation in flight and led to first commercial flight in 1919. People could now travel cross-country and globally in a speedy fashion.

1939

WORLD'S FAIR

Attendees of the 1939 World's Fair have the option of dining at Le Restaurant du Pavillon de France, operated by Henri Soule, a legendary restaurateur. The concept is so successful that Soule opens La Pavillon in 1941, serving elevated French fare in Manhattan. This is the country's first example of a pop-up restaurant becoming a brick and mortar space.

1926
MICHELIN GUIDE

The Michelin tire company begins assigning stars to restaurants covered in their "Michelin Guide." These ratings by anonymous diners served as a way of encouraging customers to drive more. More driving=more tires sold!

1945
WORLD WAR II ENDS

When soldiers return home from war, they crave the tastes they had abroad thereby popularizing these dishes in the United States. i.e.- pizza.

1956
INTERSTATE HIGHWAY ACT

President Eisenhower signs the Federal-Aid Highway Act which integrates existing turnpikes and toll highways into one interstate system, making it easier to travel by car across the country.

1973

1969

FIRST CONCORDE FLIGHT FEATURES "NOUVELLE CUISINE"

Concorde flights, which can travel from London to New York in 3.5 hours, serve in-flight meals created by chefs like Paul Bocuse, Michel Guerard and others. The term is coined by food writers to describe a new wave of French cooking employed by contemporary chefs; less complicated, fresh, simple and light, it's a complete departure from heavy dishes and cooking techniques of previous decades.

FEDEX INCORPORATES

FedEx begins transporting packages cross country via trucks. In 1973 they began shipping packages via aircraft, meaning products can be overnighted. Chefs all over the country have access to global products.

1971

ALICE WATERS OPENS CHEZ PANISSE

Alice Waters and some friends open Chez Panisse in Berkeley, California. Waters serves a nightly menu that features locally and organically grown produce and sustainable meat and seafood.

1982

SPAIN'S SOCIALIST PARTY ABANDONS MARXIST IDEOLOGY

The Spanish Socialist Workers Party wins an election and Spain joins NATO, signaling the fall of Franco-era socialism. Capital is dispersed among the Spanish.

1984

FERRAN ADRIA STARTS WORKING AT EL BULLI

Ferran Adria begins working at El Bulli in Catalonia, Spain. He eventually buys the restaurant from the owners.

1986

RAKEL IN NYC OPENS

Thomas Keller and his business partner Serge Raoul open RaKel in Manhattan serving food with American ingredients and French technique.

1987

"BLACK MONDAY" AND THE CRASH OF THE US STOCK MARKET

On October 19th 1987 the stock market plunges 508 points, the biggest single-day drop in the history of the Dow Jones, and doesn't recover for years.

2006

TWITTER IS FOUNDED

Started as a service designed to deliver your friends' status updates or "tweets" to your phone, Twitter starts and people/businesses/organizations are able to upload information in 140 characters or less to a global audience.

2007

IPHONE LAUNCHES

Unleashes 10 zillion food pics onto the world.

1995

STARBUCKS HITS THEIR EXPONENTIAL GROWTH STRIDE

As access to all the world's information becomes a plausible concept, we get our coffee on once again.

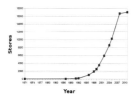

2004

NOMA RESTAURANT OPENS IN COPENHAGEN

Rene Redzepi, only 27 years old, opens Noma in a restored warehouse in Denmark, serving Nordic cuisine using only Nordic ingredients.

2004

FACEBOOK LAUNCHES

As a sophomore at Harvard, Mark Zuckerberg starts Facebook, a site designed for college students to interact with one another. That year he also introduces a "wall" feature where people can post text and pictures on their friends' pages.

2005

ALINEA RESTAURANT OPENS IN CHICAGO

Grant Achatz opens Alinea in Chicago, Illinois *sans* lobby, *sans* bar and *sans a la carte* options. He serves an 18-course tasting menu that that uses molecular gastronomy to disrupt and alter the physical composition of ingredients.

2008

ROBERTA'S OPENS

Killer pizza et al. in Bushwick, NYC's 16th Arrondissement

2015

$15 MINIMUM WAGE HITS SEATTLE

Restaurants as we know them will either cease to exist...or adapt operations to higher hourly rates through a mix of cost cutting and prices increases.

1997

GOOGLE IS INCORPORATED

Larry Page and Sergey Brin register Google.com as a domain. Their goal: a search engine that organizes the information on the internet.

2005

YOUTUBE IS INTRODUCED

Three former PayPal employees start a videosharing website and the first video, "Me at the Zoo" is uploaded. Users begin uploading videos and can view videos from all over the world.

George Deli, Amsterdam

THE CHANGING ROLES

RETAIL IN THE EXPERIENCE ECONOMY

by ANN PETERMANS, BIE PLEVOETS & KOENRAAD VAN CLEEMPOEL

Introduction

When B. Joseph Pine II and James H. Gilmore introduced the concept of 'Experience Economy' in the disciplines of economy and management in 1998, they considered 'the company' as the reference point in the company-customer relationship. In their initial top-down approach to the experience economy, individual consumers were considered as passive partakers, while companies presumed to 'know what was best' for the customer. This approach was soon criticized, because it seemed to have propelled (over) commercialization and consumerism. Hence, in what was labelled the 'second generation experience economy,' the focus shifted to dialogue for addressing customers' needs and wants. 'Customer relationship management' and the 'co-creation of meaningful experiences' became new concepts. At present, we see an evolution towards a third generation experience economy, where virtual or physical communities of consumers bond together around a particular field of interest, completely apart from manufacturers. In this third phase, the power is in the hands of the customer, and the top-down approach of the first generation experience economy has been reversed. In 15 years, the role of adaptive reuse in the experience economy has completely changed. Therefore in this paper, we elaborate the different meanings and roles that adaptive reuse has had and can have in the domain of interior architecture in general, and retail design in particular, as it relates to a particular phase of the experience economy. A selection of Western European cases is used to illustrate our point-of-view in this respect.

Reusing buildings in the experience economy Changing perspectives

Since the end of the 1990s and certainly at the beginning of the twenty-first century, a combination of economic, cultural and societal developments, technological advancements, and rise in Western prosperity have opened minds to experience thinking and experience design. In an era of increasing homogenization in diverse domains of the economy, manufacturers were obliged to break the prevailing perception of homogeneity among Western peoples. In the quest for differentiation strategies inspiration was found in the retail industry. As a consequence, the beginning of the new millennium witnessed the transformation of city centers, streets, airports, stations, museums, financial institutions, health care and many other institutions to mechanisms of shopping.[1,2] In this paper we elaborate in general design concepts that came to the forefront from the new millennium onwards in the field of retail design, an important subdomain of interior architecture. More particularly, we look at the 'usage' that retailers and retail designers have made of 'adaptive reuse' when developing retail design concepts, and its changing role in the last 15 years.

Retail design and adaptive reuse

In the experience economy, consumers look for personal, intuitive relationships with brands, retailers and relevant stakeholders in various domains of the global economy.[3] Since experiences have become integral to market logic, the designing of retail environments in the last decade has been directed towards creating atmospheres that trigger memorable and personal customer experiences.[4] The adaptive reuse of historically or architecturally significant buildings can be highly meaningful in this respect.[5] Reusing such buildings can have various advantages, not only to differentiate from competitors[6], but as sustainable design.[7]

In what follows, we elaborate on the iterations of the adaptive reuse process through the evolving concept of the experience economy to date.

Adaptive reuse in the first generation experience economy: *'we know what's best for you!'*

In the first generation of the experience economy, the design of customer experience was an autonomous decision of the company. At the turn of the millennium, many high-end brands working in this line of thought looked for historically or architecturally significant buildings in city centers, as they aimed to 'use' architecture and interior architecture as a tool for retail differentiation.[8]

The interior spaces of such retail concepts were designed without taking into account the needs, aspirations and desires of the customer. Apart from consumer-oriented considerations, re-using buildings for retail purposes also brought about its attendant challenges. There are various examples at hand of spaces that were not reused with the appropriate amount of respect for the host space.

An example of such a project is Shopping Stadsfeestzaal in Antwerp (Belgium), a shopping center located in the former city celebration hall. The building was constructed between 1905 and 1910 in a neoclassical style and is located in what is today the most important retail area in the city. When the building became underused in the 1990s, the city searched for a new use. Given its location and suitability for retail, the building was sold to a developer. The shopping center opened in 2007.

The building was in a very poor state when the restoration and renovation work started. Nevertheless, the project included an extensive restoration of the structure of the building as well as the interior decoration. Indeed, the luxurious, neoclassical architecture and interior of the building had to give this shopping center a unique atmosphere that would evoke an experience for attracting customers. Its website states:

> Because the restoration of the building included an eye for historical details and the creation of a special look, the Antwerp Stadsfeestzaal is not only a unique shopping centre but also a popular place for people to meet. Its illustrious past has not been forgotten but re-introduced in a new way. Cultural events, exhibitions, mini-concerts, fashion shows and competitions ensure that Shopping Stadsfeestzaal continues to attract crowds to its location in the heart of Antwerp.[9]

Nevertheless, there are shortcomings at the commercial level, as well as in the conservation of its value as a monument. Firstly, the circulation to the upper floors – elevators and escalators – is not clearly visible from the central hall of the shopping center, which resulted in the vacancy of a considerable number of shop units on the upper floor. Secondly, due to the monumental character of the building accessibility and visibility became an issue for many retailers as a result of the strict regulations on signage and branding. Thirdly, notwithstanding that many features of the building have been restored, the project failed in evoking the atmosphere of the neoclassical *Stadsfeestzaal* because of several subtle but, nevertheless, fundamental design decisions: the simplified polychromy, using yellowish colors instead of gold leaf for accentuating decorative features; the application of dynamic colored lighting; branding which is too showily applied on shop fronts; kitsch furnishing; and contemporary interventions that do not show any aesthetic relation with the host space. Moreover, the selection of retailers and brands present in Shopping Stadsfeestzaal were based on a marked study of the commercial center of Antwerp; for many of them, their brand image did not fit with the historic, luxurious character and atmosphere of the building.

Adaptive reuse in the second generation experience economy: *'let's work things out together'*

At the beginning of the twenty-first century, the company-centric approach of the first generation experience economy was criticized. Increasingly, customers demanded that retailers and designers take into account their viewpoints, their desires and aspirations when designing retail spaces.

Instead of the top-down approach consumers and companies started to actively communicate about what they wanted to 'experience.' Retailers and designers began thinking about how they could design environments that allowed people to co-create experiences that were meaningful and truly unique.

Whereas the first generation experience economy focused on the company offerings and considered experience as a true means that could be 'used' to stimulate company profitability, in the second generation experience economy consumers' search for identity has evolved into one of the cornerstones of contemporary retail marketing and design. In this phase of the experience economy, the concept of 'experience' has become a central concept in retail design, and retailers use the concept of 'authenticity' as a way to address the changes in customers' concerns.[10] As a consequence, retailers and retail designers try to appeal to customers by 'playing' with the concepts of authenticity and originality. For instance, some integrate authentic elements in their store's retail design, others design 'staged authentic' retail environments or even develop completely fake authentic environments.[11] In the second generation experience economy, adaptive reuse is still approached rather instrumentally, as a 'means' that can help to facilitate or help to create an interesting, appealing context, where the retailer and consumer together can co-create experiences.

An example is the bookstore Dominicanen (formerly Selexyz Dominicanen) in Maastricht. This bookstore is located in a thirteenth-century Gothic church which has had secular uses since the French Revolution, among which are a military depot, city celebration hall, post office and bicycle depot. Many of these functions were not respectful towards the architecture and 'sacred character' of the church. When the area surrounding the church was redeveloped as a retail area, the city of Maastricht designated the Dominican church for new use as retail.

The shell of the church was restored, as well as some valuable interior paintings. In order to facilitate the new use as a bookstore, a two floor high 'bookshelf' was built up as a black steel construction in the central nave of the church. This intervention allows one to experience the church in a completely new way: seen from

Pop-Up store Comme des Garçons Warsaw (PL)

the ground floor, this volume emphasizes the dimensions of the church, while from the upper floors, visitors can observe upclose the architectural details of the church. Indeed, host space and contemporary interior enhance one another.

Adaptive reuse in the third generation experience economy: 'I know what's best for me!'

In the third generation experience economy, consumers tend to informally 'bond together' in virtual or physical communities around a shared interest without any interaction with the concerned manufacturers or producers. The rise of those communities has certainly been stimulated by the technological developments over the past few decades. The rapid widespread use of the internet and social media, in combination with the development of different kinds of mobile devices, stimulate people to 'let the world know' what they think, feel and experience at various moments of the day with various products in a diverse range of environments.[12]

When looking at the approach towards adaptive reuse and its relation to retail design change is clear in this phase of the experience economy in comparison to the other phases of the experience economy. While in the first generation (and also for a large part in the second generation), retailers and retail designers approached adaptive reuse rather instrumentally, retailers in the third generation of the experience economy often try to differentiate from competitors by looking for a retail location outside the commercial heart of the city. As such, consumers are enticed to take up an even more active role than that in the second generation experience economy. Today, retailers and retail designers look for interesting sites in distant locations, which they re-use for a well-chosen, delineated period of time, often for pop-up stores or events. Here, they approach adaptive reuse from a different viewpoint and link it to ecological considerations and issues of sustainability, aspects valued highly today.

A retailer that has taken a pioneer role in reusing unique buildings and locations for pop-up stores is the avant-garde fashion line Comme des Garçons.[13] Their first temporary store opened in Berlin in 2004, and soon after they opened guerilla stores in off-beat, vibrant and marginal areas all over the world. They typically use unique, existing buildings and, instead of making large changes to them, they use the spaces as they are.[14]

A more recent long term development of a heritage site is 'De Nieuwe Eiffel' in Maastricht (The Netherlands), a redevelopment plan for one of the former industrial buildings from Sphinx ceramics.

Instead of applying a 'traditional' heritage approach, with a thorough restoration of the building, a detailed master plan describing a new program, a fixed budget and strict timing, this project starts from the building in its current state, only carrying out maintenance and repair that is absolutely necessary for safeguarding the building and its users. Next, a number of commercial functions will be introduced in the existing structure, with minimal investment. As soon as income is generated, it will be invested in further development and upgrading of the building.

A first function that will be brought into 'De Nieuwe Eiffel' is a nightclub in the basement. Next, the ground floor will be reused as a market hall, and the first floor as a HUP – a communal office space. On the second floor, a hotel will be organized. This hotel will start as a 0 star hotel, offering no more than a bed and a shower in the morning, and as such will need only limited investment. The top floor is used as a place for urban farming. The renovation of the façade will be carried out gradually and will make use of an installation for the cleaning of the glazing instead of scaffolding. As such the façade will be renovated before the parts of the building that are in use and this renovation becomes a quasi 'artwork', creating exposure for the project.

'De Nieuwe Eiffel' allows consumers to take an active role in the redevelopment of a heritage building, through which people may feel engaged, and which eventually may regenerate store loyalty.[15]

Conclusion

In this paper, we've pointed towards the different meanings and roles that adaptive reuse has had in the various phases of the experience economy. Over the three phases, the approach towards adaptive reuse has evolved from being a true instrumental 'means' that retailers and designers use to trigger experiences, to becoming a 'goal' of design. Here, due to larger societal and ecological considerations retailers communicate to consumers how they deliberately 'choose' adaptive reuse when developing design concepts. Such a deliberate choice radiates a developer's conscious vision and values towards the public.

In our viewpoint, retail concepts and approaches towards adaptive reuse are evolving more and more towards tactics of the 2nd and 3rd phases of the experience economy, which differ from the instrumental approach recognizable in the 1st generation of the experience economy.

Taking into account the enormous stock of abandoned historical buildings that is 'available' for reuse, especially in various Western countries, there are many opportunities at hand. At the same time, there is also the necessity to reuse these buildings for reasons of sustainability, historical continuity and socio-cultural connectivity.

These challenges and opportunities are certainly not limited to the reuse of buildings for retail purposes. There are many other domains – such as commercial projects and social, cultural or educational projects - for which the reuse of buildings can be highly relevant and

interesting. Also in these domains, the different phases of the experience economy can offer inspiration with regards to adaptive reuse.

After all, retailers and designers need to always take into account that designers can never create experience via adaptive reuse. Via adaptive reuse, they can only *create* the best possible "*circumstances*" to trigger experiences.

ENDNOTES

1 Petermans, Ann. "Retail Design in the Experience Economy: Conceptualizing and 'Measuring' Customer Experiences in Retail Environments." PhD diss., Hasselt University, 2012.

2 Cha, T., C. Chung, J. Gunter, D. Herman, H. Hosoya, S. Leong, K. Matsushita, J. McMorrough, J. Palop-Casado, M. Schaefer, T Vinh, S. Weiss, and L. Wyman. "Shopping. Harvard Project on the city." In *Mutations. Harvard Project on the city 1*, edited by R. Koolhaas, S. Boeri, S. Kwinter, N. Tazi, and H. Obrist, 124-184. Köln: Taschen, 2001.

3 Pine, Joseph B., and James H. Gilmore. *The Experience Economy - Work is theatre and every business a stage*. Boston: Harvard Business School Press, 1999.

4 Petermans, Ann, and Koenraad Van Cleempoel. "Designing a retail store environ-ment for the mature market: a European perspective." *Journal of Interior Design* 35(2) (2010): 21-36. DOI: 10.1111/j.1939-1668.2009.01036.x.

5 Plevoets, Bie. "Retail-Reuse: an interior view on adaptive reuse of buildings." PhD diss., Hasselt University, 2014.

6 Plevoets, Bie, Ann Petermans, and Koenraad Van Cleempoel. "(Re)using historic buildings as a retail differentiation strategy." In *Heritage 2012*, edited by R. Amoêda, S. Lira, and C. Pinheiro, 985-993. Porto: Green Lines Institute, 2012.

7 Plevoets, Bie, and Koenraad Van Cleempoel. "Creating sustainable retail interiors through reuse of historic buildings." *Interiors: design, architecture, culture* 3(3) (2012): 271-293. DOI: http://dx.doi.org/10.2752/204191212X13470263747031.

8 Klingmann, Anna. *Brandscapes. Architecture in the experience economy.* Cambridge: The MIT Press, 2007.

9 Shopping Stadsfeestzaal. "Our aim". Accessed September 24, 2014. http://stadsfeestzaal.com/en/our-aim/.

10 Lindgreen, Adam and Michael B. Beverland. "Hush, it's a secret: how trappist breweries create and maintain images of authenticity using customer experiences." In *Memorable customer experiences. A research anthology*, edited by Adam Lind-green, Joëlle Vanhamme, and Michael B. Beverland, 61-86. Burlington: Gower Publishing Company, 2009.

11 Plevoets, Bie, Ann Petermans, and Koenraad Van Cleempoel. "Developing a theoretical framework for understanding (staged) authentic retail settings in relation to the current experience economy." Paper presented at Design Research Society Conference, Montreal, Canada, July 7-9, 2010.

12 Ibid.

13 Trendwatching. "Pop-up Retail." Last modified in 2004. Accessed November 16, 2011. http:// trendwatching.com/trends/POPUP_RETAIL.htm () ; Dowdy, C. *One-off Independent Retail Design.* London: Laurence King Publishing, 2008 ; Guerrilla-store. "Guerrilla Marketing – a Trend Made In Japan." Last modified in 2009. Accessed November 17, 2011. http://www.guerrilla-store. com/ ().

14 Van Cleempoel, Koenraad. "The Relationship between Contemporary Art and Retail Design." Paper presented at Places and Themes of Interior, Milan, October 1–3, 2008.

15 Stelwagen, H., Bloemen, P., Petit, J., de Waal Malefijt, C., Pedroli, M., and J. Kemerink. "De Nieuwe Eiffel. Haalbaarheidstudie Eiffel gebouw Ma astricht", 2013.

POSTINDUSTRIAL SPECTACLE

RECONNECTING IMAGE AND FUNCTION

by **PATRICK RUGGIERO, JR.**

Replacing an Industry

The decline of manufacturing industry in rustbelt cities has led municipal governments and real-estate investors to look to tourism and entertainment as new engines of economic growth and recovery. With major producers of tax revenue and jobs now defunct, stakeholders are taking active ownership in both the rebranding and reprogramming of deteriorated properties at the heart of their towns. The emerging design work in many of these redevelopment sites straddles the interests of both developers and the public—*"Retain our heritage, but attract people to create jobs and spend money."* The resultant urban environments capitalize on the *image* of industry in a fetishized, spectacular way, using it as a billboard to attract business.

With entertainment and commerce as core programs, redevelopment offers a destination where tourists and residents alike can escape their everyday life in an environment that is exciting and in contrast to the realities of the everyday. These sites contain a unique opportunity to leverage the machines of industry within contemporary culture's obsession with the spectacle. By creating a simulated environment based on authenticity, these sites engage visitors through a false notion that what they see is real. Like the experience of a reality TV show or overzealous advertisement, one knows that the steel company, mill, or factory is no longer in business. However, through the signs and images presented the visitor is caught up in the latent memories of the industrial.

A successful simulation of this type of environment requires an array of signs, representations, and simulacra that points to the activity of an activated social

"SoMA: The Simulator of Mechanized Authenticity"

scene. For architecture to accomplish this, the uneasy relationship between how things appear and how they function must be considered. On one hand, the architectural language and ornamentation recall the past, addressing the dormant memories of the local culture. On the other hand, the buildings must function in a contemporary commercial role. In this context, form and function are no longer related—*the image* rules all as an applicable face to commerce. What these industrial sites miss, however, is the opportunity to connect image and content in a more sophisticated and recursive relationship.

Connecting Image and Content

While spectacle cannot be avoided, my project, *"The Simulator of Mechanized Authenticity" (SoMA)* reconsiders the missed opportunity to relate the image (architectural imagery) and content (function) in reuse urbanisms. *SoMA* distinguishes itself by putting forth a spectacular

image that contains many potential readings. Through the use of irony—contradictions between content and image—as well as the sampling and integration of historical and contextual precedents, the production of these connections serves as a generative means of developing a discourse and solving the architectural problems of site.

The Redevelopment of the Bethlehem Steel Site

The Bethlehem Steel Corporation, headquartered in Bethlehem, Pennsylvania, was once the world's largest producer of steel, producing the first railroads and, later, structures like the Golden Gate Bridge and the Empire State Building. After failing to upgrade technologically and suffering from complex issues with labor unions, the company officially closed its doors in 1995, leaving behind one of the largest brownfield sites in the world. The city is in the process of redeveloping the ten-acre campus that includes over 20 structures.

City planning officials have publicized a three-staged planning strategy for the redevelopment of the site that includes 1) increasing commerce with entertainment venues, 2) anchoring the commerce with business tenants, and 3) re-zoning in order to create residential housing that will support the other programs.

Situated at the center of town, most of the site is within walking distance of large neighborhoods of former working class housing in the South Side of Bethlehem. In 2006, the Las Vegas Sands Corporation purchased the site and began the construction of The Sands Casino Resort, which would necessitate cleaning up large swaths of land that were otherwise unusable due to toxic waste. Enticed by tax incentives, the Casino has gifted parcels to arts organizations, designated areas as public plazas, and constructed a convention and events center. High-profile commercial tenants are anticipated to occupy renovated building shells.

While the built (and planned) work tries to honor the heritage aspect of the site, perhaps it is obsessed with these acts of recall: theatrical lights illuminate the buildings as backdrops for concert venues; shells of industrially purposed structures are renovated for non-related uses; undeveloped buildings are fenced off and strictly guarded; and new construction features exposed materials and structure. It is as if these elements conspire to imply the continued existence of the steel company. While simulating social activity, these elements create a mask of distraction unrelated to the function of each building. Functioning at the campus scale, these simulacra become integrated into the site's context and local vernacular.

What's the problem with this? Why shouldn't Bethlehem celebrate the company that its parents, grandparents, and relatives grew up in? Naturally, the accommodation of heritage is positive, there are two critical reasons to address this phenomenon. The first is to in-

Fenced off buildings litter the redevelopment campus

sure the campus' integration with the existing city fabric, and the second to introduce a framing of the industrial imagery that avoids a mask of inauthenticity.

Integrated Context

One of the parcels that was gifted to the city by the Sands Casino has recently been deemed "The 21st Century Town Square." This new civic center is characterized by a plaza and concert shell, and is backed by four iconic blast furnaces. The plaza is host to all major civic activities including mayoral addresses and city festivals, and the site adopts the trends of similar redevelopment sites that are engineered to attract consumers. But Bethlehem's 21st Century Town Square lacks framing devices—a way to alert the occupant that the site is not meant to be read as reality.

Such framing mechanisms are used in places such as Las Vegas, a mirage in the middle of the desert that perverts the basic reality of themed localities; Disneyworld, a complete contrast to reality, which is reached on its own highway after progressing through lines, gates, and fees; and Venice, an island with as many tourists daily as there are permanent residents, which reflects a basic reality of a Renaissance town. Jean Baudrillard, in his essay *"Simulacra and Simulation"*[1] elaborates these three types of experiences, focusing on the way they use simulacra to convey various understandings of "the real." He goes on to describe a fourth type of experience, dissimulated inauthenticity (read: a state of denial), whereby the signs and images of a site mask the fact that something is no longer there. The industrial simulation in Bethlehem is that of Baudrillard's fourth type of simulation, one that contributes to a denial of the fact that its major industry has left.

Reconnecting

In order to shift the site's understanding of authenticity toward the experiences of Disney, Las Vegas, and Venice and to avoid Baudrillard's dissimulated inauthenticity newly implemented design must frame the imagery. While on a macro level this framing would interrupt the integration with the site and town, a building-specific critical framing would alert visitors that what is going on in Bethlehem is extraordinary.

This is where *SoMA* interjects to create value in commercial mixed-use real estate. The project proposes a series of renovations that reconsider the relationship between the architectural image of reused buildings and their programmatic function. A commentary on both the spectacularization of architectural imagery and an exploration into the potential of architectural representation, the project demonstrates how a richer, framed reading of spectacle can contribute to reclaimed urban environments. Each of the project's five buildings seeks to simulate, in its entirety, a previously existing condition. The form, material and architectural language all serve as simulacra, or signs/evidence to support this. The project differentiates itself from the site's existing context by producing a framed understanding that the spectacular experience is manufactured, establishing the connection between image and content.

The Stage | Transformation

The Stage takes a critical stance towards Bethlehem's fascination with lighting—projecting onto, making backdrops of, and illuminating the ruined buildings of the steel company. The building is programmatically divided into three distinct parts: the Seating Area, the Point of Purchase (POP) Facade, and The Back-of-House. Materially, *The Stage* contrasts the projected image and formed concrete that is smooth and unfinished—a canvas for the temporal expression of false ruin. A crane structure spans the Queue Pad and POP Facade, supporting lighting and projection equipment that sporadically projects a ruin texture onto the concrete, giving the area a ghostly sense of being of another time. The ephemeral quality of *The Stage's* image is contrasted with the hardness of its detailing. Its action is sporadic and natural. Like Yellowstone's Old Faithful, it runs on its own schedule and cycles in an unpredictable fashion.

The formal organization of *The Stage* is a machine for commerce: waiting line, service counter, and back of house. Its attraction is the spectacle of a ruin projected onto a new construction. *The Stage* honors the history of the site through a reverberation of readings. While discernibly produced of modern construction techniques, the form recalls what could have been a staging yard for forged components awaiting shipment.

The Tower | Hyperbole

The Tower is a critique of Bethlehem's rush to enclose, partition off, and preserve any building remains for as long as possible—even in the face of their eventual destruction. Fenced off and condemned buildings litter the redevelopment campus, establishing a landscape of inaccessibility and surveillance. *The Tower* is a nine-story office building, built of steel, glass, fencing, walls, and barriers. Each floor contains a full luxury office suite with 270° views of the Bethlehem Steel Campus. At the ground floor, the tower is enclosed with existing walls and security fencing systems. *The Tower* will be the premier office space in the second phase of the city's redevelopment.

The Tower borrows the architectural language of the iconic blast furnaces. Conveyed as Bethlehem Ironworks' first building of the 19th century, *The Tower* honors the history of the site by blurring new and old. While constructed with modern techniques and means, the

building's language vacillates between contemporary building systems and iconic artifact. *The Tower* frames itself through the unrelenting use of barriers, enclosures, partitions and fencing. This amplification of an existing phenomenon conveys its inauthenticity.

Prototype

Both *The Tower* and *The Stage* seek to combine commerce and heritage in the critical framing of spectacle as intervention in the Bethlehem Steel Redevelopment Campus. Each does this in different ways: while *The Stage* produces an ephemeral reading that is temporal and transformative, *The Tower* establishes its permanence through layers of security and hyperbole. Both aim to engage consumers with a nuanced reversal of their understanding of authenticity. The interventions use spectacle to both honor heritage and fuel commerce.

SoMA is a prototypical project: a test for addressing the redevelopment of sites involving heritage and the reuse of multiple culturally significant buildings. *SoMA* exemplifies an opportunity to develop ordinances and guidelines for designers, connecting the imagery with the programmatic use and content of each proposed building.

CATHEDRALS OF CONSUMERISM

EXPERIENCING CORPORATE INTERIORS AND BRANDS

by S Y L V I A L E Y D E C K E R

A space is exciting as an experience of all the senses: visual, acoustic, haptic and other impressions combine to create a multi-sensory, holistic experience. It is an experience that is perceived consciously, but experienced subconsciously. If spatial experiences are not to be left to chance, as so often happens, they need to be designed purposefully. Today Interior Designers in a wide range of different fields and branches target the senses, filtering the information to be communicated, and turning spaces into communicative elements that build bridges between the sender and the recipient.

The term spatial experience conjures up images of spectacular productions in spaces of the kind created for world expos, in which the visitor is catapulted from one surprise to the next, each space a veritable firework of spatial experiences for entertaining the visitor. The experience of space takes on the character of an event, carefully orchestrated to impress and enthrall the visitor at every step. In addition to the visual impression of the colours and materials, elaborate film, sound and light installations are employed to reinforce a desired effect.

Innovative interactions, for example illuminated surfaces that respond to movement through the use of sensor-controlled walls of OLEDs, create an atmosphere that transports the visitor into another world. Other worlds are also being created using virtual reality, which adds a whole new dimension to spatial experience that enriches the real environment. Users are no longer in the here and now but experience something completely new in an artificially created parallel world. Despite their technical sophistication, these are as yet no match for the "real" experience. There is a perceptible shift towards interaction using IT-based approaches that capitalise on the fact that people are social beings for whom interaction is a vital part of life. In short, whether primitive or high-tech, the aspect of interaction is an inseparable element of communicative spaces. Interaction therefore forms the basis for experiencing space.

Economic interest

The aspect of spatial experience of most interest to companies from an economic perspective is the potential they offer for branding.[1] They can enrich the design of corporate interiors in such a way that the brand identity is experienced in three dimensions. The more compelling the experience, the stronger the impression of corporate identity. With sensitivity and the necessary know-how it is possible to successfully invest spaces with a character that is appropriate to the company and that matches the company's brand values and corporate identity (CI). The better it appeals to our senses, the more it activates the multi-sensory potential in each of us. The initial impetus for creating such spaces is derived from the profit-oriented motives of the corporate marketing department.

Corporate spatial experiences are usually those that are in the public eye, and it is these spaces that are the focus of corporate design and corporate interiors. They

Experiencing Outdoor - an indoor recreation bistro-area for staff

communicate a desired image and serve as a powerful marketing tool for transporting brand identity. As such they are ideal for showrooms, for reception spaces and conference rooms within offices that serve a hospitality function for visitors to the company.

Whether a simple boutique, an exclusive showroom or a prominent flagship store, the creation of a shopping experience has long been an effective means of increasing sales and of turning casual shoppers into loyal customers. Glamorous flagship stores, such as those of Prada in New York or Hermès in Paris, are designed as centres of attention and in turn become meccas for entire communities of fashion-conscious shoppers. Showrooms, such as those of Apple, are temples of brand culture, embodying the brand values and establishing a sense of brand attachment. Shopping malls likewise go to great lengths to create extraordinary shopping experiences, enticing consumers with all manner of entertainment offerings so that visits to these cathedrals of product consumerism become recreational outings to be undertaken again and again. All these are examples of customer retention at its best.

Lifestyle and branding
The lifestyle associated with a brand likewise plays an ever greater role, which explains the spread of brands across multiple segments from fashion to products and living accessories to music and modes of movement and transport. The brand environment becomes an overarching identity, and with it the associated spaces which make use of myriad facets and tools to achieve their effect.

While e-commerce is without doubt flourishing, what it lacks, despite the attractions of virtual reality, are spatial experiences: e-shops are therefore used in tandem with real shops that bring the shopping experience to the real world and onto an authentic level.

Trade fair stands are a further showplace of extroverted spatial experiences. In some branches, not only the stands of individual companies but also the spaces of the trade fair center are transformed into spatial experiences to heighten the attraction of the trade fair.

Companies have also begun to recognize the value of communicating the history and/or innovative character of their brand as an educational experience, as Coca Cola and Ferrari have demonstrated to great effect with their exclusive company museums. They serve not only the job of communicating the history of a company and of cementing the tradition of its brand, but also turn it into an enjoyable first-hand experience for visitors. Ever more companies are following in the footsteps of these early trendsetters, eager to relate their own company history and not least to anchor their brand in the minds of the consumers. They take visitors on an imaginary journey through time, accompanying the brand as it evolved, all the time establishing a rapport between brand and visitor.

Workplaces as experiences

Very often corporate identity and brand are directed predominantly outwards, in stark contrast to how it is experienced from within the company. Great attention is devoted to getting the all-important first impression right – usually the reception space – while the rest of the premises is often neglected. As a strategy, this is flawed: brand values are equally important for staff, and their needs are in turn vitally important for the company's success. A company's "human resources" are one of its most valuable assets, and staff motivation increases when they identify with their company. As a shortage of skilled workers begins to set in, it will become ever more important to first attract and then retain skilled staff. The spatial experience of the workplace is a strategic factor in this objective that should not be neglected, particularly in those locations with large numbers of offices and admin centres.

People experience their employers through the spaces they are given to work in, because they reflect the attitude of the company toward them. What is important is how valued they feel, and how they experience the work they do. The space in which work is undertaken determines if it is perceived of as pleasant, process-oriented and efficient or laborious and uninspiring. Modern companies recognise the value of creating pleasant office environments that also incorporate spaces for relaxation and interaction. This ranges from the ubiquitous table-football table, comfortable lounge areas, and trendy staff canteen with outdoor terrace to conference areas with different degrees of formality and informality for varying moods and occasions.

Calm and focused spaces, often in the form of office cells, may be most appropriate for concentrated work but calm and focused does not necessarily equate to dull and uninspiring. To maximise the potential of their staff, companies should be willing to invest in pleasant work environments coupled with corresponding spatial experiences.

Remarkably, it is the tech firms on America's West Coast – Google, Facebook – that are at the forefront of a new interior trend that highlights the office environments of its workers. These large open spaces seem, at first glance, more like adventure playgrounds for leisure and recreation than workplaces, with as much focus on the fun factor as on work. But they are also expressions of the value the companies place in their staff, who were consulted for their ideas, all of which help to increase staff loyalty and work motivation. While at the end of the day this alone probably justifies the decision, the as-

sociated publicity also reinforces the reputation of the company as a responsible and concerned employer.

As the images of these office interiors circulate around the world, they contribute as part of a marketing mix to the image of the company as a forward-looking employer. This is aimed not just at the company's own staff but also at potential future employees as well as other users who value this kind of social commitment. The potential effect of this image transfer is not to be underestimated. It is less surprising, however, that the spatial environments within the tech-community are similar in design. One reason could be that the needs voiced by the staff in the various companies are essen-

Experiencing an Hommage to Fashion-Brands gives identity to each floor of an apartment building converted from an office

Hommage à

Rei

Tokio Français
Comme des garçons
Fetzen, Risse
Avantgarde
Prêt à porter

C'est qui? 誰ですか?

tially of a similar nature, leading to a similar end result. In terms of creating a unique brand identity, however, this is far from ideal. The spatial experience of such corporate interiors should also reflect the specific brand identity of the company, rather than that of a generic tech company, where one cannot tell if it is an industry giant or small start-up.

Whether it is the "hey, we're cool and creative" interior of "Google's playground" or another atmospheric variant that is perhaps more conservative, more elegant, more discreet or more homely, what they all share is the wish to create spaces in which the people who use them can feel comfortable. The "playground", for example, conjures up images of children who need little more than their fertile fantasy to turn more or less anything into an incredible adventure. The elderly have a similar capacity for fantasy: in geriatric care, biographic therapy has been used successfully to help people with dementia recall their own personal history and biography. Images of famous people – Elvis Presley, Elizabeth Taylor and others – or objects, smells and activities are used to evoke particular memories. They help recall past experiences, which help people to live happily in the present with the help of the past.

Motivating brain scripts

Spaces can be used to motivate particular brain scripts, by using a certain sound, smell or a combination thereof, to awaken associations with roots in subjective human experience. Sometimes a particular sound or smell sets off a film in the mind's eye. Neuropsychological marketing is aimed specifically at this aspect. The effectiveness of this method has been proven by conducting MRT (magnetic resonance tomography) scans on test subjects, in place of the conventional user survey. By measuring brain activity with the help of MRTs, scientists can ascertain the precise reactions of these subjects. Brain research into the reasons why these reactions occur is already underway but at present is still in the early stages of what promises to be an exciting investigation.

Through the collection, anâlysis and linking of ever increasing amounts of data, we are gaining an ever better picture of how we respond and behave. One's personal behaviour is analysed and predicted, sometimes even before one knows what one will do next. Manipulative and controlling mechanisms hook into our behaviour patterns and attempt to steer them. The more we commit our lives and experiences to the digital realm, the more we contribute to this mechanism, benefitting companies by helping them place their advertising with ever greater accuracy. The over analysis of every aspect of everyday life allows reason and rationale to dominate how we live our lives, reducing the room for fun, chaos, and simply fooling around. Authentic feelings and normality run the risk of falling by the wayside in an ever-present pressure to achieve perfection in which normal,

Red creates a sense of power and activity in the lobby of an apartment-building

authentic situations are perceived of as being imperfect or somehow sub-standard.

Stimulation and enjoyment

In the context of a gradual shift away from the need for ownership to a willingness for collective sharing, experience begins to acquire a different quality and meaning. Instead of purchasing products, society purchases experiences. This has implications for spaces, which per se are inseparably intertwined with living and quality of life. An experience is coupled with time, and which of those is more valuable? In a world of faster-higher-better-further, do things always have to be spectacular? Can they not be measured and discrete? And can that not make an impression for precisely that reason? Can they stimulate our senses gently, can they emanate, leave room for thought, for emotional connection with

the place? Balance is needed, not only in the right places but also at the right time.

For branding and corporate interiors, companies wishing to make a lasting consumer impression are beginning to turn to experience marketing, in which the right experience is provided at the right time. Brands and their worlds, brand environments and their lifestyle just need to match. So, by all means let us dive into a world of spatial experiences, but let us also withdraw from time to time into the contemplative atmosphere of a pleasantly designed, peaceful environment. A place where we can simply enjoy.

ENDNOTES

1 Leydecker, Sylvia. *Corporate Interiors*, Avedition, Stuttgart, 2014, p.272.

Hugo Gernsback wearing TV Glasses

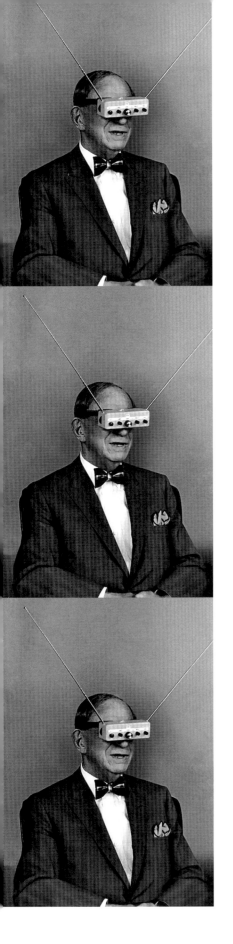

MORE OF SOMETHING ELSE

CONJECTURE ONE-THIRTY (TU)

by JEFFRY BURCHARD

Buildings are slow

Buildings emerge after a period of toil. They hunker down in the world as the physical manifestations of disparate ideas. Exhibiting the requisite firmness of structure, resilience, and financial benefit, buildings are slow to accept fundamental change. Their existence is as a background to experience. At best, buildings are instigators of action or co-conspirators of transgression. At worst, they are nothing but the places where everything takes place.

Experience is fast

Experiences come and go with the flicker of the phone's flash. Experience as a temporal event in a continuum is axiomatic. But today Technology Ubiquitous (TU) sponsors experiences that seem to lap us and any remaining desire to be inert. TU actively works against stability. It purports organized chaos, posing as clouds, as the agile and dexterous cures to the humdrum and to the alleged curse of settled opinion. Everything can be exactly what it is and what it is not, simultaneously[1].

Function is not static

The manifestation of architecture, as constructed building, is an act of enabling unforeseen experience.

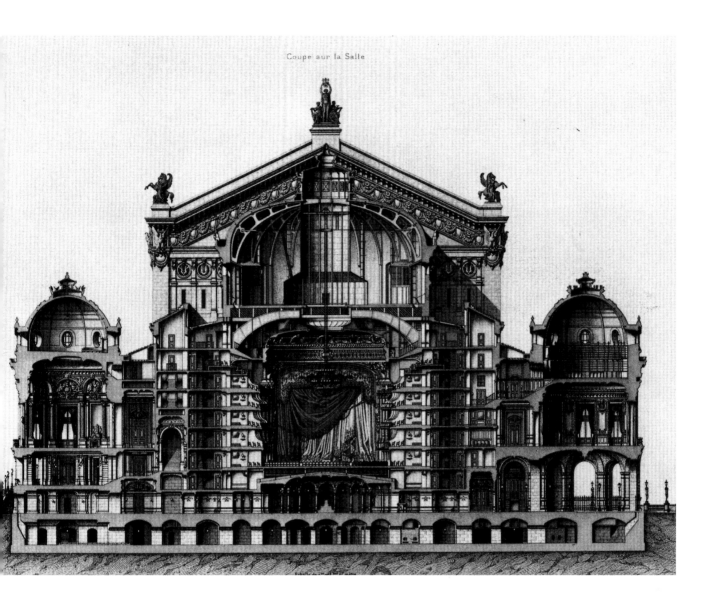

Coupe sur la Salle

A building can be designed for something, but some other things will always happen there, despite the work's best effort to enforce a particular function.

We could designate buildings according to their amiability to future functional transformation. Some would be buildings that might be made to do *more of* what they were originally intended to do, and some are buildings that might do *something else*.

Narrow or severely restricted possibilities for functional transformation can often be attributed to type-specific architecture, in which use and form create a tautology broken only by the most resolute architectural transgression. Both the Paris Opera House and a Wendy's Restaurant are prime examples: the particular function of each is inherently tied up in the specificities of the building's form. At the Paris Opera House, sequential building containers that scale vertically, but not horizontally, are inextricably linked to the generic and particular functions of the opera. But the forms also guarantee an ideal experience, one of unbelievable opulence that extends the aura of the opera into the lobby, prolonging the fantastic, and delaying confrontation with the boredom beyond. A Wendy's Restaurant is as specific as the Opera, its entire operation concerned with efficiency and the projection of average. Food delivery is expedited through careful and calibrated relationships of drive-through, kitchen prep, and cash register. A "resolute architectural transgression" would be a Paris Opera in a Wendy's or a drive-through in the Opera. Feast your imagination on that spectacle.

Other buildings, too, are susceptible to functional transformation. Grand Central Station is as splendid an entrance as one can have into New York City. Built explicitly for commuters arriving from the northern suburbs, the building has always provided amenities for the comers and goers in the basement and at the edges. But the Main Concourse, the cavernous and clearly defined waiting room for metro passengers, has sponsored plenty of additional functions. These include an American ballistic missile exhibition, a flash-mob, and an open Apple store. This space is flexible precisely because it is large and open like a floor in an office building. There the space between core and window waits for the next successful enterprise to place its temporary stamp of branded occupancy.

Form is not stable

One error in the dialectic between form and function is the false assumption that one is more stable that the other. We know that function is not static. Architectural form, even as the physical manifestation of building, is not stable. Actions, transgressions, readings, and other everyday uses compel architecture—and the quest to define the relationships of the forms, spurred by infinite motivation—to persist beyond initial construction.

Forms are malleable in at least three ways: physical alteration, appropriation, and illusion. The first demands quantitative change, the second depends on a redefinition of existing formal relationships, and the third exploits that schism in architecture between cognition and perception. The next portion of this essay focuses on illusion as a means to perceptibly achieve alteration.

Surface Deception

Trompe l'oeil is the technique of producing three-dimensional perspectival depth on a two-dimensional surface. As an artistic technique it dates to antiquity, but for architecture it comes of age in the 15th through 17th centuries when some buildings found that they were constrained by site and construction. These constraints might have prevented the development of buildings that could not correctly achieve the demands of type during the Renaissance or the demands of the exuberant form of the Baroque.

An early example of trompe l'oeil in architecture is the Church at Santa Maria presso San Satiro, designed by Bramante in the late 15th century. The church, owing to its type-specific heritage, required a choir[2]. There was no room for this space on the site, which was constrained by an unmovable road. In order to create the sense of depth and thus the appearance of formal correctness and functional purpose, Bramante introduced an illusion. He had a trompe l'oeil painting of a perspectivally correct choir applied to the wall behind the altar so that from some points of view there appears to be a proper extension of the nave.

In the mid-17th century, Orazio Grassi built the Church of St. Ignatius of Loyola at the Campus Martius in Rome. This church employs a trompe l'oeil painting in the ceiling of the nave that distorts the flatness of the ceiling and obscures the corner where wall meets ceiling, giving the appearance of a glorious volume extend-

ing to the heavens. A more profound use of the technique is at the ceiling of the crossing, where a distorted painting replaces the actual geometry of the requisite vault. A hole, akin to the opening in the Pantheon, is seen at the top of the "dome." Surprise, there is no dome.

It is worth noting that in both of these works there is a double force at play – one that permits you to see something that is not there and one that forces you to assume a singular position for the illusion to work.

Still Learning.

In Las Vegas, the singular position gives way to relative positions. A singular position demands absolute relationships for the illusion/deception to work, whereas relative positions require only relative relationships. At St. Ignatius one must stand on the bronze circle for the trompe l'oeil to succeed. In Las Vegas one must just be somewhere, anywhere really, from the city street to the bedroom, for the effect of Las Vegas—the total obfuscation of boredom—to have potent agency. The sky painted over the interior canal at the Venetian, the casino floor,

Exhibition of the first American Ballistic Missile in the Main Concourse at Grand Central

the oasis, and the roof-top roller coaster all safeguard against the view of anything else.

The streets of Las Vegas have vacillated between singular and relative positions for the experiences of VEGAS to achieve their intended dysphoria. In the 1972 seminal book, *Learning From Las Vegas*, Denise Scott Brown and Robert Venturi reveal the real force behind architectural image in an experience economy: competition.[3] The Casinos first developed strategies to rebrand or reassert themselves in the increasing noise of the strip by renovating, replacing, and enlarging their facades and signage. At some point this armature of architecture was too slow, and not visible to passing cars, so the façade moved perpendicular to the street in the guise of a billboard. This was the perfect place—stripped of all architectural ambition other than the forces of economy and automobile traffic—for the quick changeover of graphics that compelled people to experience this or that casino. Retail immediately joined in the fun. The billboard's numbers grew exponentially until a bottle of sun tanning lotion was equivalent to the main show. Everything was lost in a sea of magnificent sameness. The buildings became signs, but they grew too large to become the place of quick rebranding. Their enormous presence would have to dominate. The advantage was given to relative positioning in order for the experience to achieve full effectiveness... when in Vegas it is clear that you are not anywhere else.

Video Mapping

Recently, two projections onto contemporary buildings continued the project of trompe l'oeil and the competing contemporary interests in temporality and original iconic form.

In 2011 the production company Tali Yaacobi produced an art-video mapping for the Tel Aviv Museum of Art[4]. The video was shown at the museum's opening. The animated trompe l'oeil capitalized on the precise formal geometries of this complex building designed by Preston Scott Cohen. In the most convincing moments the video-mapping was aligned with the seams of the physical panels in order to radically alter the appearance of the building. Possible alternative methods of design generation were suggested that might be more akin to Llebeus Woods or Igloo construction than to Cohen. Formal coherence and clarity were challenged as new functions were generated: ballet dancers pirouetted in an occupiable *brise soleil*. The experience was produced through deception, but the effect was spectacular due to the specificity of the building's form and the skin's original function. It is this confrontation of cognition and perception that made the work so important.

In 2013, John Ensor Parker projection-mapped the Wiley Theater[5], an architecturally interesting box designed by Joshua Prince Ramus of REX and OMA. The projection capitalized on the blankness of the canvas

Fresco with the apotheosis of St. Ignatius, church of Sant'Ignazio, Rome

Screen shots from the video mapping of the Tel Aviv Museum of Art

and produced less formal transformation and more generic digital art. However, as at Tel Aviv, this mapping was most convincing when it toyed with the stable state of its architectural host, particularly when the structural guts of the building were revealed through a translucent skin.

In both projects the function of the façade was expanded to include illusion as an experience. The specificity of either form is rendered both insignificant and entirely necessary.

Augmentation

Augmented Reality is sweeping digital culture[6]. It holds promise for an engagement with the static and subdued qualities of constructed architecture. It could allow for radical transformations of existing forms. It could disengage function and form and encourage the forces of individual desire and entertainment.

What if illusion's requirement for singular position and relative position was replaced by individual position? Could we imagine an individual donning a prosthetic that altered the entirety of daily experience through the perceptual appropriation of form? Could the technology be so powerful that the physical properties of the

background remained unimportant? Or could architecture be designed with limitless perceptual overlays?

The originality of wearable augmented reality is its capacity for personalization. Trompe l'oeil in the churches required singular positions but the effect was lost, if not made humorously evident, to the congregation at large. In Las Vegas you can be anywhere and it happens. With wearable augmented reality and user reactive augmentation, the adjustment of perception can work at the location of any individual, anywhere, and for every individual at the same time: a kind of Mona Lisa on acid.

Ducks and Sheds for Conjecture

Returning to *Learning from Las Vegas*[7] we can now say that everything can be a decorated shed. Ducks may no longer exist. Video-mapping has an apparent (though untested) ability to decorate and transform the perceptible image of a building, rendering even the duckiest duck a banal background. Architecture has thus come full circle. It is background—the place where everything else takes place.

In Times Square, the surrender of all building surfaces to advertising produces a unique experience

Screen shot from the video mapping of the Wiley Theater

often accepted as entertainment. Existing surfaces are unapologetically re-used. The augmentation of reality vis-à-vis the billboard is both a visual illusion and a mental construct. The brain must confront a double paradox. The content on display is fake and the feelings associated with the product are imaginations, but entertainment often occurs at the edge of imagination and actuality.

Epilogue

An argument for the continued specificity of architectural form is that the potential of Technology Ubiquitous in architecture is not one of significant change to architecture, but a reification of the banal condition of architecture as building. It has persisted since the dawn of the discipline. The notion that the specificity of architecture is incompatible with the forces of the present is entirely false. Architecture is in a perfect position to engage those transitory concerns and interests. It is a mistake to disengage or to wallow in the self-pity that assumes that all things fast and entertaining are more consequential than the slow, sometimes tedious, production and life of architecture as buildings.

ENDNOTES

1 Simultaneity is perhaps best explained by the "Law of Contradiction." The law says that contradictory statements cannot be true in the same sense at the same time. But if either sense or time are NOT the same, then both statements can be true.

2 In churches the "Choir" is the extension of the central nave, the primary main aisle, beyond the transepts crossing.

3 Venturi, Robert. et al., *Learning from Las Vegas*, (MIT Press, 1977), 6-9.

4 *Locomotion*, Tel Aviv Museum of Art Opening Ceremony Video Mapping Projection (Tali Yacobi Productions, 2011).

5 Parker, John Ensor. *Blueprints & Perspective*, (2013).

6 Two examples: 1) The company Oculus, a start-up company that manufactures vitual reality headsets used to augment realistic experience, was recently sold to Facebook for $2 billion USD. 2) Various universities have created centers, departments, and degrees, among them the Augmented Reality Center at Miami University.

7 Venturi et al., Learning…, 88.

Screen shot from the video mapping of the Wiley Theater

Public Camping, Public Design Festival by Esterni, 2011 (photo@Delfino Legnani)

ALTERNATE HOSPITALITY

A NEW FRONTIER

by TIZIANO AGLIERI RINELLA

In contemporary design and architecture, the Experience Economy has had increasing significance, especially in specific fields and design categories such as hospitality or exhibition design, where its fundamental role is habitually and widely acknowledged. The forthcoming Expo[1] 2015 in Milan, scheduled to open in May and expected to draw over 20 million visitors and 150 participants from all over the world, is one such example.

The Expo, specifically focused on the visitor experience, will not be just an exhibition but a process of active participation among a large number of players on the theme of "Feeding the Planet, Energy for Life". Unlike the typical trade fair (an exposition of products to purchase, addressed to businessmen or buyers), Expo is a quasi theme park for adults, children and families that will contain "attractions" instead of simple fair pavilions. Visitors will instead experience a unique journey that will focus on the complex theme of nutrition, with the possibility of taking a trip around the world, sampling the food and traditions of people from all over the globe.

A new generation of designers of innovative *food experiences*[2], like the ones created by the Dutch eating designer Marije Vogelzang, the British architects Bompass & Parr or the Spanish food designer Marti Guixé, as well as the Italian group *Arabeschi di Latte*, is expected to present their original interactive projects in Milan.

The Expo theme of "Feeding the Planet, Energy for Life" is also broadly connected to the concept of "sus-

shows, etc.) where the offered experience has the ability to generate substantial income for the overall regional and national economy. These events attract great numbers of visitors, every year, not only for the specific commercial purpose of the single fair/event, but for the equally attractive experience offered by the multitude of related events, cocktails, parties, free concerts and shows, generated in the whole city.

As Pine and Gilmore asserted[3] , hospitality is a field in which the experience economy has traditionally been a fundamental issue. In the hotel, definitely, the single guest's overall experience equates to more than the simple service of accommodation. From the arrival at the hotel, the reception service at the front desk, to the guestroom's equipment and comfort - all must be in perfect order to fulfill the guests' expectations and foster their loyalty. Hotel managers recognize that today's guest is, however, not simply looking for a place to sleep, but seeks a unique and memorable experience that has been at the origin of the rise and success of design boutique hotels[4] . Recent trends increasingly demand a relational hospitality where guests search beyond the inner aesthetic experience to a social and interactive one.

According to the designer Werner Aisslinger[5] , a hotel in an urban context nowadays demands more contents and storytelling, connecting guests with the city. In his 25hours Bikini Hotel in Berlin, guests start to experience their travel destination when they first step into the hotel, meeting local inhabitants, as this inspiring and connected place also attracts the local scene. The theme of the hotel is the "urban jungle", a very local and Berlin-oriented design story: it is not far from the famous Berlin nightclub *Dschungel* (Jungle) and from the renowned Berlin Zoo, icon of the city's cinematographic imagination. Its design concept is oriented to a young and dynamic generation of travellers: less space for luggage and more for bathrooms, sound systems with Bluetooth, social public spaces with power supply(for smartphones and laptops), authentic locally-sourced materials and city-bicycles for rent.

It is important to recognize the relevance of the experiential and the social in new affordable hospitality typologies. In new hospitality models, importance placed on the experience given to the guest leads to solutions that favor "people interaction". In recent years, there has been a rise of new hospitality forms offered by the Internet and social networks that have significantly increased such opportunities to communicate and interact amongst travellers, allowing them to access information by comparing other people's experiences[6]. Websites such as Tripadvisor, apps, travel blogs and virtual communities broaden the "experiential menus" proposed to the various guests and encourage the creation of new hospitality forms outside the established system of accommodation models. Sites such as Airbnb, Couchsurfing or Campinmygarden aim to put potential users in private homes or

tainability", not only through food, but the environment, energy and natural resources. The set of experiences addressing these themes is the engine of the experience economy that will produce significant and widespread income. According to economic predictions, the cost of the Expo (estimated at 1,2 billion euros) will be entirely covered by the revenue generated by ticket sales, royalties and profits on purchases inside the exposition area, and from the 19 international sponsorships.

Today's Expos differ dramatically from the Universal Exposition of the XIX and XX centuries. With the global development in the last decades of media and Internet, the public has little interest in discovering the achievements of the latest technologies. As a result, since 2000, Expos, from being universal fairs, have been transformed into theme parks. The new Expo as a type is characterized by a charged admission, the presence of hundreds of attractions, food, beverage, merchandising, and a programme of scheduled events – all of which resemble the family of experience venues such as casinos, cruises and amusement parks. At Expo 2015, what will be sold to the public is the overall "experience" of living a unique event, which will involve not only the proper Expo area but also the whole city of Milan and its surrounding urban area.

Hospitality is one of the business segments more strictly related to the experience economy in the induced consumption of Expo that will encompass the whole city and the surrounding territories. The city of Milan has a long-standing tradition of international events (the many international trade fairs, design and fashion weeks, art

Sharing dinner **by Marije Vogelzang, Tokyo, 2008** (photo@ Kenji Masunaga)

Studio Aisslinger, 25 hours Hotel Bikini, Berlin, 2013

unusual locations. Couchsurfing, in particular, offers an exchange service of free accommodation and is, as well as Bed Sharing[7] launched in 2007 for the Design Week in Milan, a model of alternative hospitality that creates new opportunities for a deeper interaction between guests and hosts.

An extraordinary international event like Expo will generate a relevant need of temporary hospitality solutions, wielding a strong impact on the urban context. Accommodating a remarkable number of temporary visitors will require the city to adapt and respond to the demand for new and better public services and spaces. Facilities for accommodating visitors (meeting places, info-points, public transports and toilets) will be essential for providing quality in the sharing of experiences and in the perception of the urban venue.

Collapsible and reversible solutions, such as pop-up hotels and urban camping have gained popularity in Europe as the experimental field for the relational dynamics among event, urban venue and users[8]. Installed in open spaces or in unused buildings, these temporary structures offer inexpensive solutions for accommodating a new generation of savvy travelers, seeking real contact with the local context from a perspective of sharing

spaces, services and personal experience. The short implementation times of these solutions allow visitors to be accommodated for limited periods in outdoor areas regained by the urban landscape or indoor, inside unused or underused buildings. These parts of the city, often forgotten by the local inhabitants, are reused activating a perceptive change.

In Milan, this result has already been achieved in recent years by the project Public Camping of 2011, for the Public Design Festival by Esterni, taking place every year during the Design Week. Set up in two different locations of the Lambrate zone, outdoor under a road bridge and indoor inside the building of the Lambretto Art Project, this temporary urban camping was equipped with a full list of facilities, such as a relax-meeting area and an international library, internet point, workstation, lockers room, restrooms and toilets all of which enhance the guests' experience through creating shared opportunities.

The materials used are light and, in some cases, recycled or reusable, to enable high levels of flexibility in shaping the spaces for rest and personal care as well as the collective ones for meeting, eating and drinking. Once the event is over, the camping is dismantled, its

EXA structures, **YES WE CAMP!, Marseille European Capital of Culture 2013**
(photo@Sébastien Normand)

components recycled and the space restored to its initial condition. Thus, this kind of accommodation represents a sustainable approach to temporary hospitality, significantly reducing the impact on the urban context.

Another interesting reference project is EXA structures, installed by the organization YES WE CAMP! for the event Marseille European Capital of Culture 2013. This temporary, urban camping is built by both locals and international visitors in a joint architectural performance. Its modular, no-waste approach is an expression of the architecture of a new breed of urban nomads, providing sleeping and chilling shelters while at the same time opening up new ways of public space re-appropriation.

The peculiarity of this project is that Hexa Structures require little construction skills, due to their standardized and optimized elements consisting of wooden palettes and steel scaffolding. Construction can be fast and easily mounted using low-tech fastening techniques. In the proper conditions, a whole camping facility for hundreds of people can be built or dismantled in a very short time. Both activities are energizing, bringing peers together, and creating a shared experience.

Furthermore, this venue also provides a social space: it hosts the ever-changing, fluid, temporary interrelational contacts created between people, whether traveling, constructing, chilling or sleeping in the Hexa Structures. In this project, the beauty of the structures lies less in the aesthetic than in the formal expression of the way of living of its temporary inhabitants.

At international events such as Expo 2015 with the allied activities of augmented hospitality demand, the whole urban and suburban venue is an opportunity for temporary "experience design", fulfilling the main design principles suggested by Pine and Gilmore[9]. Though ever evolving with time, one constant remains at Expo Milan: the design must conform to the format of the *Bureau International des Expositions* (BIE) and especially to the compulsory rule that the exhibition area, after having been built and "experienced", must, at the Expo's conclusion, be completely demolished. This rule makes the visitor experience "unique" and unrepeatable and provides an incentive for interested visitors to visit Milan during the Expo, as after the closing date of October 2015, only the Italian pavilion *Palazzo Italia* will remain. Limited in time and not replicable, the universal EXPO format of the BIE can nowadays certainly be considered one of the most effective and innovative models of the new frontiers of the Experience Economy.

ENDNOTES

1 Collina, L. "Expo 2015. Un laboratorio ambientale", in *Milano. Laboratorio del moderno*, Innesti/grafting, catalogo della 14° Mostra Internazionale di Architettura, Biennale di Venezia, vol.2, Marsilio, 2014. p.119.

2 Aglieri Rinella, T. *Food Experience, design e architettura di interni*, Postmediabooks, Milan, 2014.

3 B.J. Pine and J.H. Gilmore, op.cit.

4 Aglieri Rinella, T. *Hotel Design*, Marsilio, Venice, 2011.

5 "Interview with Werner Aisslinger", in *Ottagono* n. 270, May 2014, p.52-53.

6 Scullica, F. "Online hospitality: an Italian excellence: new scenarios", in *Ottagono* n. 270, May 2014, p. 39.

7 http://www.bedsharing.org

8 Algani, E. "Pop-up hospitality for events", in *Ottagono* n. 270, May 2014, p. 56-57.

9 The five design principles are: theme the experience, harmonize impressions with positive cues, eliminate negative cues, mix in memorabilia and engage the five senses. Pine, B.J. and Gilmore, J. H., op.cit., p. 102.

EXA structures, YES WE CAMP!, Marseille European Capital of Culture 2013
(photo@Sébastien Normand)

Public Camping, Public Design Festival by Esterni, 2011
(photo@Guglielmo Trupia)

BIKINI BERLIN

BECOMING AN ICON OF
POST-WAR RECONSTRUCTION

by DIONYS OTTL

Beginning with a building planned with the outmoded norms of the 1950s, strict historic preservation requirements, and a construction site in the middle of Berlin wedged between the Berlin Zoo and the arterial roads *Budapester Strasse* and *Kurfuerstendamm*, the conditions for revitalisation were complicated. Yet it was this combination of existing building conditions, location, and an intelligent extension that make the transformation of "Bikini Berlin" such a success story. Officially inaugurated in April 2014, the advertising now promises "shopping experiences for tomorrow's urban society," an "innovative hotel experience," and a "grand cinematic experience!" [1]. The unique architecture of this building forms the foundation of these experiences and restaged this important urban area.

In 2002, Bayerische Hausbau GmbH und Co KG bought the historically protected ensemble consisting of the "Bikinihaus" opposite the Memorial Church *(Gedaechtniskirche)*, the "large skyscraper" *(großes Hochhaus)* at Hardenberg Square, the cinema *"Zoopalast"*, the "small skyscraper" *(kleines Hochhaus)*, and the multistory car park at *"Elefantentor"*. These buildings were the starting point for the development of an urban center comprising a hotel, cinema, shopping mall, and offices. In 2012, the Berlin office of Hild und K Architekten was commissioned for this ambitious undertaking. They were asked to rework the master plan by SAQ architects

in order to relate it to the requirements of the monument conservation act (Deutsche Stiftung Denkmalschutz).

The objective was to make the lightness of the period in which it was built palpable in the context of the colorful and international Berlin metropolis.

The architects Paul Schwebes and Hans Schozsberger originally designed the "Zentrum am Zoo," a clean and transparent ensemble. It was symbolic of the post-war economic upsurge and a milestone in the creative resurgence of the Federal Republic of Germany.

Its centerpiece, the "Bikinihaus," has since become an icon of the post-war reconstruction period. In the course of the revitalisation measures, the original façade was reconstructed so that the vibrancy of the building, which had badly deteriorated over the years, became evident. Projections and recesses in the reinforced concrete, with remarkable bands of delicate windows and glass balustrades, gave the outer skin of the former textile center of West Berlin a light, almost woven appearance. Current strict energy-saving regulations made transfer-

ring the elegance of the profiles and the original color scheme, typical of the 1950s, a complicated task. The open mezzanine, which had been closed off in 1978, reappeared.

Particular care was also taken to reconstruct the south facade of the "small skyscraper." Built as an office building, it now houses a design hotel. A suitable alternative for the exposed concrete surfaces required quite a bit of patience and endurance.

The restaging of history was not limited to the reconstruction, but was incorporated into the materiality of the new facades: reconstruction work required replacing some historic constructions and materials. One example is the colored glass panels on the old facades. In order to create historical continuity, the original glass facades were shredded and added to the new building parts, endowing them with a glittering sparkle. The plasterwork recreates the plasticity of folded material, like the gathers in a summer dress, and the old building materials have come to life again. The new facades give rise to associations, a dialogue between the buildings' new uses and their history.

Besides staging the history of the building and its connections to the birth of the Federal Republic of Germany, the architecture also puts this historic location back into the limelight. Constructed in 1862, Berlin's "new west" was a place of entertainment in the "golden twenties," a meeting place for artists and intellectuals, and a direct competitor to *Potsdamer Platz* and *Alexanderplatz*. When the *Kurfuerstendamm* was extended to become a 53-meter-wide avenue modelled on Parisian boulevards and the *Kaufhaus des Westens* was opened in 1907 at Wittenberg Square, it became a popular shopping area and soon filled with cafes, restaurants, boutiques, theatres, cinemas, and galleries. The objective of the reconstruction of the "Zoo district," which had been largely destroyed during the Second World War, was to create a symbol for the economic miracle. During the period when Berlin was divided, the "City West" became the centre of the free city and monopolized the social and economic life of the time. The desire for rebuilding, which for political reasons focused on this area, was expressed in the now revitalised building ensemble. The stellar "Zoo Palast" cinema, with approximately 1,700 seats and now reopened, became a legendary cinema in the 1950s. From 1957 to 1999, it screened the main films of the Berlinale and was the venue for the Golden and Silver Bear awards. The cinema was a "window to the West" at the interface of two political systems. After the fall of the Berlin Wall, City West stepped into the shadows of the then booming construction areas in the former East Berlin. However, since 2010, investors and urban planners have rediscovered City West. The neighboring Zoo, which houses the largest variety of species in the world, and the famous Memorial Church, rebuilt in 1961, have always been

popular destinations for Berliners and tourists alike. The Church, with its spire still in ruins, has been a landmark of the western part of the city for decades.

These meaningful surroundings are once again placed in focus. There is a landscaped terrace garden of approximately 7,000 square meters on the rooftop of the newly built concept mall open to the public. The terrace is reachable via a stadium-like flight of stairs on the inside and a large open flight of stairs leading from the forecourt at Budapester Strass from the outside. By building over the former delivery yard between the Bikinihaus and the Zoo, a bridge is created between the pulsating city life on the one side and the large open

TOP
The new landscaped terrace garden

BOTTOM
Bikini Budapesterstrasse

areas of the Zoo on the other. The spectacular views from the terrace have attracted thousands of visitors since it's opening.

The interior design of the mall also relates the urban hustle-and-bustle of City West to the natural environment of the Zoo. It is no coincidence that the leading metaphor is that of "the great bridge." This association is reinforced by the steel beams that dominate the large three-part hall on the ground floor. The hall opens to the north with a 4 x 14 meter window that looks onto the neighboring zoo where baboons squat on their "ape rock." The interior, in shades of green, makes direct reference to the Zoo while, as a continuation of Breitscheidplatz, the pavement of the square reaches into the building.

The special location between the Zoo and the center of the city serves as a marketing argument for the design hotel which says that it's "open for monkey business" and is "as wild as a jungle."[2] The architectural handling of the facades of the building is done in the same spirit. In order to maintain the lively handcrafted character of the south facade, meticulous care was taken to search for suitable systems for the reconstruction of the concrete at the narrow sides of the building.

Similarly, the historical choice of colors—with which the architects had originally alluded to the then new architecture of Le Corbusier and Gropius—was not questioned when reconstructing the ensemble. In fact, it inspired the color concept, allowing the north facade facing the Zoo, with its floor to ceiling glass walls, to relate to the surroundings. Each respective hotel room has French windows so the guests can experience the Zoo close up with all its impressions, noises, and smells. Another of the distinctive architectural features is the entrance hall, which at over eight meters high allows the ground, first, and second floors to melt into one another to form an atrium flooded with light. The atmosphere is that of a gallery, flanked by two supports at the entrance that are still inscribed with original graffiti. The spirit and history of the place is intact.

The "Concept Mall," housed in the lower floors of the "Bikinihaus," is "a compilation of carefully curated and coordinated boutiques, concept and flagship stores, as well as gastronomy offers and service providers."[3] These high demands on quality, individuality, and authenticity were also the leitmotiv for the interior design of the retail areas. Steel beams that are exposed in the three-part hall on the ground floor cannot usually be spotted in conventional shopping centers. Massive oak planks frame the large bench at the window overlooking the zoo and cover the open stairway to the roof terrace. The gallery floor is laid with cobble-wood flooring made of oak. The facade of each of the shops is designed as a flexible system of varied glass formats and structures. The raw steel frames were simply waxed. The reinforced concrete ceiling of the hall remains raw and emphasizes the lighting elements, which were custom designed for the building.

"Bikini Berlin" can be seen as a positive example of the beneficial interplay between the interests of investors and the preservation of historical monuments. When the "experience economy" allows for such projects, we architects see it as a welcome venture.

ENDNOTES

1 https://www.bikiniberlin.de/en/bikini_berlin/what_is_bikini_berlin/
2 http://www.25hours-hotels.com/en/bikini/home/home.html
3 https://www.bikiniberlin.de/en/bikini_berlin/what_is_bikini_berlin/concept_mall_1/

The mall is conceived of as "the great bridge"

Aerial view of the theme park "Huis ten Bosch" in Sasebo, Japan

GOING DUTCH

DUPLICATION, AUTHENTICITY
AND REPROGRAMMED EXPERIENCE

by IRIS MACH

Huis ten Bosch is an idyllic coastal town, which would pass as the perfect historic Dutch city except for its location in Omura bay, on the Japanese seaside. The fact that it was conceived as a theme park might diminish the antagonism, but reducing it to this function reveals only a small part of a complex story, which ranges from an industrial landfill to an ambitious theme park and finally to a possible role model for the city of the future.

Dejima

"Why Dutch"? The answer dates back to the year 1600, when the first Dutch ship called "Liefde" ("Charity" or "Love") arrived in the town of Usuki on the island of Kyushu in southern Japan. This was the start of a long-term relationship in trade and cultural exchange that would last for hundreds of years.

However, the relations between Japan and Europe became strained through Portuguese traders, Christians who had arrived in Japan earlier and begun to proselytize to the displeasure of the Japanese military ruler. The ensuing conflict led to a 1614 ban of Christianity and further restrictions to European traders, finally resulting in a complete closure of Japan ("sakoku") from 1641 to 1853. The only Western country allowed to maintain limited contact with Japan during this time was Holland, due to its military support of the shogun against the Christian rebels. Even so, their trading post was banned to an artificial island in the port of Nagasaki, called "Dejima", which was connected to mainland Japan by only one strictly guarded bridge.

Despite this confinement, the cultural and technological exchange was considerable and gave rise to a spread of Dutch knowledge in many fields such as weaponry, machinery, geography, natural sciences and medicine, which made the Netherlands the most influential Western country in Japan for more than 200 years.

After the Meiji Restoration, Japan successfully transformed itself into a modern nation, becoming one of the world's leading countries in a remarkably short period of time. One of the principal reasons that Japan was able to achieve such success was that even during the self imposed isolation of the Edo Period, Japan maintained some contact with Western civilization through its trade with the Netherlands. In this way, the Netherlands played an important role in the modern history of Japan. However, the Japanese public is almost completely unaware of, and lacks an appreciation for these contributions.[1]

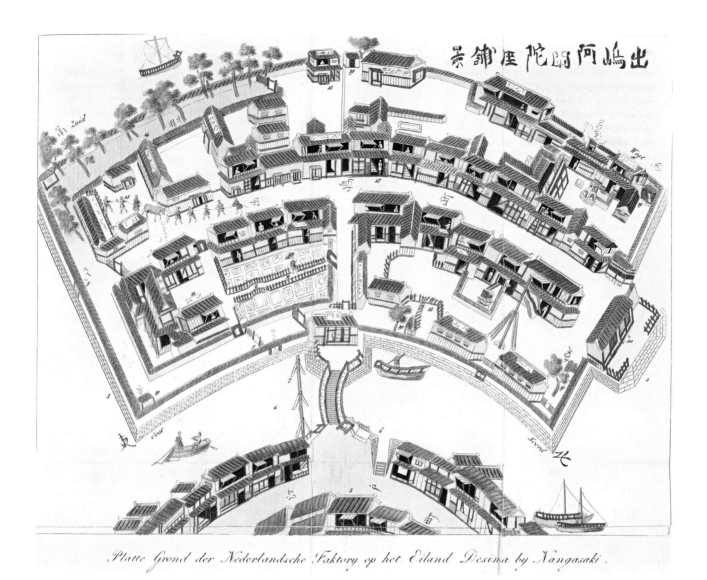

景舗前陀蘭和嶋出

Platte Grond der Nederlandsche Faktory op het Eiland Desina by Nangasaki.

Hollander Village

Based upon the long-standing connection and cultural exchange, a so-called "Hollander Village" was established in 1983 in Sasebo to celebrate the reciprocal relationship between the two countries through an "edutainment" facility. This concept was already well established in Japan in the form of several so called "gaikoku mura" or "foreign village" theme parks, which provided both leisure and the experience of a journey abroad, though within a safe environment and without the hardship and unpredictability of actual travel. [2]

The success of "Hollander Village" led to an expansion five years later, in 1988. For the project, a seaside property in Omura bay, close to Sasebo city, was chosen. The focus of the new park was instead on "authentic" Dutch landscape, culture and atmosphere. Its goal was not only recreation but the creation of awareness for the importance of the Dutch culture in Japanese history.

Huis ten Bosch

In developing the new theme park, Yoshikuni Kamichika, CEO of Huis ten Bosch, aimed not just to present but to re-enact the formation of a historic Dutch settlement on the artificial island of Dejima. In this regard, the building site itself offered a good opportunity: as a former industrial landfill, it had similar properties to the polder landscape in the Netherlands and therefore also required comparable technical measures for its cultivation. Furthermore, both the quality of the soil and the bordering bay water proved a severe ecological challenge. As such, it was decided that the project should strive beyond the scope of a theme park and become a showcase for ecological town planning.

Under the lead of Kamichika and the support of project director Dr. Takekuni Ikeda, the building ground - at152 ha almost the size of Monaco (195 ha) – became an experimental laboratory for the planners. The seem-

Imagined bird's-eye view of Dejima's layout and structures (copied from a woodblock print) by Toshimaya Bunjiemon of 1780 and published in Isaac Titsingh's *Bijzonderheden over Japan* (1824/25).

ingly contradictory aim was to design a Dutch city in the style of the 17th century, yet featuring 20th century knowledge and technology for ecological building.

Instant History

To achieve maximum authenticity, the planning team invented a fictitious history for a prototypical dike and dam town and developed the settlement according to this timeline. The instant history starts in the 12th century with a fishing village at a river mouth to the sea. From the 12th to 14th century, it develops into a small city with an inner and outer harbor, churches, a city hall and a city wall with a gate as a protection against enemies. Between the 14th and 17th century another enclosing wall with bastions is added. In the 17th century, during an economic boom, warehouses for the "East Asia Trading Company" and the eponymous palace "Huis ten Bosch" are erected. Throughout another economic revival in the 19th century, the port expands and some annex buildings were added to the royal palace. Finally, in the 20th century, holiday houses are built alongside a new canal, trees are planted and the trading harbor is transformed into a marina for sailing boats. This imaginary historical development was communicated through seeming changes in the buildings, such as walled-in window openings and mended pavements, as well as some "adaptive reuse" of the buildings.

Theming

Organized as an experiential space, the basic structure consists of five "landscapes" with differing atmospheric qualities: namely Old town, New town, Port town, rural area and forest. These were further sub-divided into ten "cityscapes", based on typical Dutch towns or places: Breukelen, Kinderdijk, Nieuwstad, Museumstad, Binnenstad, Utrecht, Spakenburg, Forest Park, Palace Huis ten Bosch and Wassenaar.

These areas were covered with about 150 simulacra of Dutch architecture, out of which 12 were exact replicas of well-known landmark-buildings (e.g. Utrecht cathedral and Gouda city hall) and another 16 almost identical duplicates with small changes in size or detail, mostly clad in original Dutch bricks specifically import-

ed from the Netherlands. Their placement corresponds to cityscapes and with a visual sequence (Welcome view, Nature view, City view, Harbor view, Royal view), designed to guide the visitors intuitively through the park.

Reprogramming

Despite these efforts, the objective of the project was not simply to imitate or present the architecture and culture of the Netherlands. Although Huis ten Bosch consists of buildings in the Dutch style, according to Dr. Ikeda, the leading architect, the park in fact epitomizes the concepts of Edo (= traditional Tokyo) while using the Netherlands only as a formal model.

In the spirit of the popular motto "wakon yôsai" (Japanese spirit and Western technology), this mixture of Japanese and Dutch knowledge is evident also in the composition of the planning team, which consisted of a group of Dutch experts responsible for the "hardware" (architecture and urban planning, garden and landscape design, material sciences, road planning, bridge and canal construction) and a group of Japanese experts in "software" fields (history, art, psychology and sociology).

In this sense, the act of copying was not just one of duplication, but, in fact, learning through the process of reproduction and finally assimilation by combining with Japanese ideas – a concept that had already been successfully implemented by the Japanese post-war industry in the fields of automobile industry and electronics.

"We commenced the HUIS TEN BOSCH Project in Nagasaki Holland Village with the traditional Japanese spirit of reverence for Nature in our hearts. Although we basically used Dutch architecture as a model, we tried to build a town based on the manners and concepts of the city of Edo. To successfully accomplish our task, we applied the most advanced technology. Using today's Holland as a model had tremendous significance as we not only fulfilled the concept of our project, but we were also fortunate to learn many new things.[3]"

Corresponding to this principle, several of the buildings were "rededicated" in adjustment to the requirements of the theme park and thus became hybrids with a traditional Dutch façade and a modern (partly Japanese) interior. For instance, the Amsterdam railway

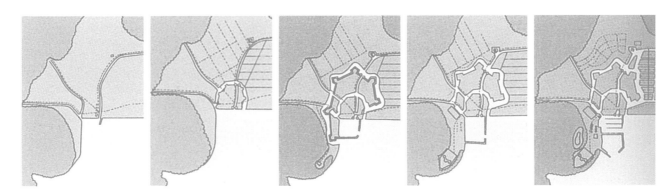

Fictitious development of the settlement "Huis ten Bosch" in Omura Bay, Japan from 12th to 20th century.
1 - Fishing village
2 - Small city with inner and outer harbor
3 - Additional of another canal, bastions and the "Huis ten Bosch" palace
4 - Enlargement of harbor and palace
5 - Addition of holiday houses and marina

station was converted into a hotel, the Gouda city hall to a museum, one housing complex was "reused" as a shopping mall and another adapted to a hotel with a navigable courtyard in the example of the traditional Japanese waterfront teahouses.

This procedure was justified by the common process of converting historic buildings in Europe, which often commands the preservation of the outer shell of a protected monument while changing the original function. By this method, the Dutch image became the "hardware", which was reprogrammed to run under a Japanese "software".

Soundscape

In striving to extend the scope beyond that of a typical theme park – the developers of Huis ten Bosch intended for the antithesis of the typical overpopulated, chaotic, polluted and noisy contemporary Japanese city. As an aesthetic experience, it also offered the opportunity for visual and acoustic recreation. While it is quite common to hear e.g. the tape-recorded sound of birds as a soothing background noise in Japanese train stations, the designers of Huis ten Bosch did not want to support this kind of "schizophonia", but decided to take a more holistic approach.

A design team comprised not only of architects and landscape planners, but also experts in lighting and sound-design began the process with a documentation of the existing soundscape by a 24-hour recording of the acoustic environment, in spring and autumn respectively. Additionally, several experiments measuring the sound propagation in the area were conducted. Based on this data, the existing noises were contrasted with the desired sound scenario and measures for a dramaturgical soundscape redesign were taken. On the one hand, this meant the reduction of noise pollution through e.g. speed limits for cars, restrictions to engine capacities and the use of signal-horns, the application of low-noise tires and a dense forest plantation against the intrusion of outer sounds - on the other hand, the enhancement of desired natural sounds by settling diverse species of birds and insects and ameliorating the corresponding ecosystems.

This natural soundscape was complemented by carefully chosen urban sounds like the chiming of the city hall bells or the clatter of horse carriages, which added to a consistent, yet varied and harmonious soundscape in accordance with the theme of "harmony between man and nature".

Total Immersion

While numerous efforts were taken to design the most coherent and authentic environment possible, the most important but also most difficult factor concerned the people themselves. The aim was to involve the visitors both mentally and physically as much as possible, in order to enhance their experience and integrate them into the concept. Further blurring the line between spectatorship and performance, hotels were located directly within the park and visitors were offered Dutch costumes during the course of their stay.

The actual aim of the developers, however, went well beyond this stage. Upon closer inspection, the park shows its true colors: an area named "Wassenaar" is set apart from the designated visitor's accessibility and contains about 250 privately owned Dutch style apartments and villas along picturesque canals. They are the beginning of a long-term plan to turn the theme park into an actual city, as soon as the enormous construction costs (close to 3 billion USD) have been amortized through entrance fees. The second and third stages of expansion envision 10.000 and 150.000 inhabitants, respectively.

In fact, part of the transformation has already taken place - Huis ten Bosch was recognized as a district of the adjacent community Sasebo and received the official suffix "-chô" in 1991 (ハウステンボス町). It even has its own train and railway station and runs a branch of the school for Japanese studies of the University of

Japanese Dutch hybrid of flower beds depicting traditional "ukiyo-e" (Japanese woodblock prints)

model of a Dutch city. Rather, it will be an unquestioned symbol of traditional Japan.[5]

Thus, what started with the arrival of a Dutch ship in Japan some 400 years ago, may come to its ultimate conclusion by means of a theme park becoming an actual settlement: the total immersion and assimilation of Dutch culture in Japan.

PS:

Due to several economic crises in Japan and the following decline of visitors, the Huis ten Bosch theme park had to file for bankruptcy in 2003 and was taken over by Nomura Principal Finance Co. until 2010. The current holder is H.I.S., a large internationally operating Japanese travel agency, which finally reported a raise in visitor numbers and a financial gain in 2013. Though the company plans to add gambling facilities and a shopping mall to the park in order to improve the financial returns, there still seem to be plans to open at least part of the park area to the public, following Kamichika's original idea.

Leiden, receiving annually about 20 Dutch scholarship students, all of which simultaneously contribute to the authentic Dutch atmosphere, and further diminish the boundaries between staged entertainment and real education facility.

What began as a theme park facility for short-term entertainment and temporary escapism is changing into a real-time, lifelong experience facility, and even a role model for future city planning. As Kamichika points out: *Huis ten Bosch was designed in this vein, as an experiment on a grand scale of the city of the future.*[4]

While it may seem far fetched to regard a medieval Dutch city as an archetype for future Japanese town planning, the project initiators see the development in fact as a continuation and renewal of an ancient Japanese tradition:

Kyoto's urban planning was originally modeled after ancient Xian. After 1,000 years, it had ceased to be the copy of anything. It had become the unequivocal symbol of ancient Japan. Cities are consummated by their inhabitants through the culture they create. 1,000 years from now, no one will dare say that Huis ten Bosch is the

ENDNOTES

1 Ikeda, Takekuni. "The Spirit of the HUIS TEN BOSCH Project" in *Huis Ten Bosch. Design Concept and its Development.* (Tokyo: Nihon Sekkei and Kodansha, 1994), 8.

2 A study of MIT conducted in 1997 counted 21 "gaikoku mura" among a total of 65 theme parks in Japan.

3 Ikeda, Takekuni. "The Spirit of the HUIS TEN BOSCH Project" in *Huis Ten Bosch. Design Concept and its Development.* (Tokyo: Nihon Sekkei and Kodansha, 1994), 10.

4 Kamichika, Yoshikuni. *"Building a Town for the Millenium"* in *Huis Ten Bosch. Design Concept and its Development.* (Tokyo: Nihon Sekkei and Kodansha, 1994), 15.

5 D'Heilly, David. "Letter from Huis Ten Bosch", *Any 1 (4)*, 56-57.

Japanese visitors of Huis ten Bosch dressed up in Dutch national costumes

View from the inside, Million Donkey Hotel © feld72

MILLION DONKEY HOTEL

AND OTHER MEMORIES OF STONE

by MICHELA BASSANELLI

Italian Small Villages: A geography in a state of abandon

I don't remember when I had for the first time the feeling that the places had their meaning, their emotions; I imagine that it happened very early in my childhood. In the land of my youth all places had names and they were special. They had a secret. There was the place of the strawberries, one of the mushrooms, the place of the chestnuts and cherries, of the water and the sand. Everyone maintained a special relationship with a particular place. (Vito Teti, *The Sense of Places*)

In the middle of the sixties, Giuseppe Chiari, the famous proponent of Fluxus, designed a performance in the small village of San Gimignano in Tuscany. For one night this place was transformed into a musical

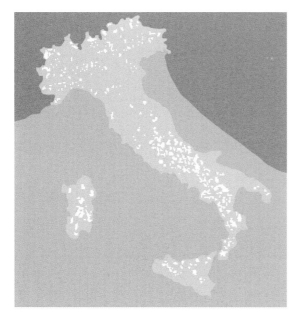

instrument, in the wake of "Suonare la città" ("To Sound the City"), 1969 by the Italian artist. Very long cords were fixed on the top of the travertine towers and pulled to the ground, while Chiari passed from one to another moving them and making them resonate. For one night San Gimignano re-activated its towers, former symbols of the city's defences, in a living theatre involving people, architectural spaces, tourists, wind, sounds and voices. A few years later, this type of artistic, temporary strategy was used by a number of initiatives as a way of thinking about contemporary architecture and the reuse of the existing built fabric.

The Italian landscape is arranged in a constellation of small villages like San Gimignano, historical hillside towns that are the symbol of a rich heritage. This landscape is etched in the faces of old men and women, in the very little streets and squares, in the hanging garden and on the walls of stone buildings. In these places there has developed a characteristic memory of practices, customs and traditions and also a typical art of inhabiting. The word "borgo" suggests an old town centre refering to municipalities that have less than 5,000 inhabitants and are characterized by its placement on the hillside. These villages are symbolic of those magical places where history seems to have stopped, and their beauty represents a minor widespread heritage—tangible and intangible.

The data emerging from the major research on the subject points out that 72% of over 8,000 Italian municipalities have fewer than 5,000 inhabitants: an Italy where 10 million citizens live, representing more than 55% of the national territory. Many of these small villages are abandoned. Others risk the same and still others are traces of past memory. Since the Second World War, through environmental disasters or for economic and demographic reasons, these centres have begun to radically decrease in population. These places can be defined as "slow territories" because they have developed a model that favours slowness and non-contamination. In some cases, the event of the abandonment was whole, and the ruins remain today as testimony to a past life. In other cases, the phenomenon has been partial, and today "slow territories" are mostly inhabited by an elderly population that is no longer able to sustain an economy.

Memory is one of the supporting elements of this situation: the place testifies to the past and the life of the people in it. Antonella Tarpino defines it as *memories of stone*: "houses of mind: between their imaginary walls hide moody feelings of memory." (Tarpino 2008, 5) The value of this heritage lies in the relationship that is generated between the future and the ruin, between past and memory. These are uncertain places[1] where abandoned walls show the sense of a space that is still active but could have a different function than what was originally conceived.

We can define this kind of heritage as "neglected cultural heritages,"—they include both artefacts, which are hardly or only recently considered in literature, as well as overlooked historical traces and remains that have lost their relationship with, and meaning for, their places and people, in the belief that their protection, revitalization and re-introduction within the system to which they belonged (or may belong) can significantly contribute to fostering sustainable local development, strengthening or re-creating inter-generational and inter-cultural relationships, and promoting the con-

LEFT
Map of the future of the Italian Small Villages.
In white are represented the cities destined to disappear
RIGHT
Ruins, Valle di Zeri, Tuscany, Italy

struction of a new sense of belonging. In response to the increasing awareness of the value of small villages, some initiatives have arisen in Italy, in particular those related to artistic and temporary actions. With the involvement of local community, these projects demonstrate the importance of protection, restoration as well as valorisation in the conservation of places and memories that would otherwise be lost. These reactivation processes are driven and facilitated mostly by arts and native crafts, intended as practices of reinvention.

Performances and temporary events as a strategy of reactivation

The concept of performance and "performativity" is developing into part of a meaningful strategy in different fields of knowledge: art, theatre, museums and even cultural heritage. In recent years, the concept of *performing heritage* (Jackson and Kidd 2011) has developed as a possible strategy to re-use patrimony: "Heritage performance has been defined as the use of theatre and theatrical techniques as a means of mediating knowledge and understanding in the context of museum education." (Jackson and Rees 2005, 304) Performing language reveals itself through different ways: from authentic theatrical representations to interpretations in the first person to artists' performances. Indeed, the word "per-

formance" refers to the execution of direct action and physical experience: a practice that involves gestures, body and new media. (Goldberg 2011) By focusing on action, the performing strategy stimulates constructive participation and learning, highlighting or bringing to light what is often neglected. This kind of strategy is closely related to the contemporary cultural transformations that require alternative forms of temporality, which perhaps emphasize mobility and migration as threads of collective identification. The concept of "performativity" is linked to that of the event in architecture, crippling every idea of expressed form through definitive arrangements and highlighting what happens and especially what can happen in any space. (Kwinter 2002) In a context characterized by the progressive distortion of the historical environment, through the globalization of economies, customs, knowledge and social composition, an active and effective protection of cultural heritage is needed. If "global networks have diminished the importance of place and traditions, ruptured boundaries and created hybrid, in-between spaces" (Graham, Howard 2008), it is necessary to reweave connections between people and places. This suturing should be done by developing new models based on the involvement of local communities, aimed at fostering cultural and economic advancement.

This type of artistic intervention implies an essential relationship between the site, the community that inhabits it and the artistic research. Focusing not so much on the production of objects as on the activation of shared processes with spectators who become co-authors and patrons, "New genre public artists draw on ideas from vanguard forms, but they add a developed sensibility about audience, social strategy, and effectiveness that is unique to visual art as we know it today." (Lacy 2010) In this essay the concept of *performing heritage* is used to indicate a possible strategy for operating within an abandoned context, which nonetheless has an important memorial value and a close link with the history of a place. Tangible and intangible objects like old traces, people and stories all contribute to creating a new temporary reuse. These little places, like small Italian villages, can no longer function as they did in the past. They require a different vision of contemporary reuse that stimulates the creation of a new economy based on temporary processes and the involvement of a local population. However, while we obviously cannot recreate a way of life that no longers exists, we can recover the universal value of memory as part of a cultural heritage to be shared with future generations.

Some experiences of performing heritage

Starting from these premises, it is possible to identify some interesting cases of reactivation through temporary events related to cultural production and artistic experimentation. A pilot experience "Borgo della Musica" ("Village of Music") of Provvidenti, a small place in the Molise region touched in 2002 by an earthquake, is a pilot experience focused on the reuse of spaces, housing and abandoned places. Deprived of their primary function, civic or social, it facilitated the livelihoods of artists and bands as a perfect place to develop ideas and projects through to production and staging of shows and concerts. This three-year experience has been central to the inhabitants of the village, who have had the opportunity to be in touch with a new reality and to see their country revive during this period. The music and the inevitable interaction it generates with the community meets all the prerequisites of a sociological study conducted between a community born of a past and a present reality on the edge.

A similar strategy was used in the historic village of Santarcangelo di Romagna, in the Emilia Romagna region. The project was initiated in 1971 and engendered a very close relationship between the city and the commissioned artistic projects. It is an event of contemporary theatre involving streets, little squares and abandoned buildings with an intensive programme for international artists. Since 2012, the association's activities are organized continuously throughout the year, giving shape to the activities aimed at nourishing the theatrical culture of the area, hosting artists in residence and building pathways for visitors to the territory. In this way the village is transformed into one big event of a living theatre, occupying various places in the small town.

A more complex project, combining several strategies for reactivating this kind of heritage, is "Paesaggio-Azione Matese," a collective programme started in 2002 with the purpose of promoting new forms of artistic expression between landscape and sustainable architecture.[2] The project is designed to stimulate new forms of cooperation, to facilitate economic development, and to promote a new perception of the territory as a dynamic resource, one that originates from the interaction of local contributions and new economic and cultural impulses. The Matese area can offer itself as an environment for the development of a new concept of landscape through experimentation of nature and pre-existing local cultures. The proposed actions comprise a series of artistic performances and interventions for landscape enhancement to be implemented in the territories and in the historical centres of five municipalities of the southern part of the Matese Regional Park: Capriati a Volturno, Fontegreca, Gallo Matese, Letino and Prata Sannita.

"Paesaggio-Azione Matese" is divided into three main interventions: Urban Node, the Villaggio dell'Arte and a Centre for Ecological Education. The first, Urban Node[3], is a multidisciplinary and multimedia laboratory for social and cultural interaction where local communities participate in the elaboration of their history using new strategies for investigating the territory. This region has been characterized by significant migratory flows

View of the bed and of the garden, Million Donkey Hotel © feld72

of populations coming from the south, north and east of Europe. One of the aims of this project is to recreate this cultural landscape by mapping the histories and memories of its inhabitants. The physical location of this liquid archive will find its place within a restored building in Gallo Matese that will house video and installations, allowing local people to interact with the work and integrate the material with their personal stories: "In this new configuration, open to histories, memories and possibilities coming from elsewhere and emerging among us, identity cannot be experienced as something given and accomplished; it becomes an opening, a continuous elaboration toward the future." (Chambers 2003, 18) This venue will also host conferences, seminars and workshops to, in a sense, become a "Laboratory of Memory."

The second intervention, Villaggio dell'Arte, is an annual collaborative event that creates an active exchange with the research done in the Urban Node and Laboratory of Memory. The resulting works are the outcome of a continuous relationship between local people, international artists and local institutions. The sites of these actions include historical centres as well as rural and mountain landscapes. From 2005 to 2006 many groups of artists produced twenty workshops and installations

Million Donkey Hotel © feld72

View from the outdoor bed, Million Donkey Hotel © feld72

with the cooperation of inhabitants who were actively involved in organizing the different events. The idea of these interventions was to create a moment of interactivity and to offer a new perception of the places around them. One of the most interesting projects, by Austrian architects feld72, is "Million Donkey Hotel" [4] located in the old village of Prata Sannita. For this location, the architects posed the question: how can one transform the lost spaces of migration into a new potential for the future, without denying its past? The idea behind the project is to conceive of the old village as a diffused hotel, which has some free rooms left: its abandoned spaces. These cells all become interconnected, and Prata Sannita changes into a space of interaction. With a very low budget of 10,000 Euro and the help of more than forty local volunteers, the formerly empty spaces were transformed into meeting places, bedrooms and rest spaces: "Occasionally they are filled with the protagonist of a new, much more contemporary kind of migration: the nomad of nowadays, the tourist, which in some moments can transform these spaces into a non-commercial version of a Hotel." (Paesesaggio Workgroup 2008: 130) This long-term intervention has focused on the creation of a greater awareness in the inhabitants of their area, looking for new ways to activate new networks and relationships.

This exchange aroused a new energy, capable of stimulating both those who live and work in these villages and those who visited it. The project generated a geography of performances where local people, artists and tourists were the principal actors. "Paesaggio-Azione Matese" was an event that activated social and economic dynamics, generating a greater visibility of these areas. In Prata Sannita, for example, the association created by the local residents is now managing visits and stays at the "Million Donkey Hotel", a new type of cultural tourism. In Gallo Matese and in Letino, new restaurants and accommodations have opened during the project. The challenge will be to continue these experiences, situating them as integral parts of the territory. The cases mentioned are just a few examples of how it is possible to reactivate these kinds of places through performative strategies that, for a limited period, are able to create new meanings and stories, while also collaborating with an existing community. In order to reweave these vital connections, the triad composed of people/place/heritage needs to find a renewed reciprocity based on strategies not only of protection but of re-activation and valorization, focused on the remains of the past and a different life in the present.

ENDNOTES

1 Augé, Marc. *Rovine e macerie. Il senso del tempo.* Torino: Bollati Boringhieri, 2004.

2 The project was coordinated by the Landscape Workgroup and was composed of six architects: Claudio Calabritto, Monica Carmen, Raffaele Esposito, Mario Party, Rosita Izzo and Orlando Lanza.

3 The project was curated in collaboration with the Centre of Postcolonial Studies at the University of Naples. "L'Orientale" was represented by Prof. Iain Chambers and Prof. Lidia Curti with the architects Monika Wisniewska and Aleksandar Cetkovic in Zurich.

4 http://www.milliondonkeyhotel.net/

+33 200

+30 000

+25 000

+22 600

+20 000

+15 000

+10 000

+5 000

DWG 003 - East Elevation

A FUTURE OF PILGRIMAGE

by ANDY LOCKYER

Technology and globalization have broken down boundaries and dissolved limitations to lifestyle and comfort, resulting in new cultural expectations of value. In a society where consumption is the primary means through which identity is established, as products and services become increasingly commonplace, enhanced forms of consumption must evolve from the old. Tourism is by no means exempt from this advance; the constant pressure to appeal to potential travellers has driven the tourism industry to operate upon a diverse frontline of defining cultural values and desires. The experience economy is the latest stage of this progress, seeking to involve travellers within a unique experience. Given that western society at large has 'suffered' a modern crisis whereby the cultural and national narratives of progress and meaning have eroded, the next phase of tourism will inevitably seek to offer travelers a reorienting experience, an opportunity to find personal meaning and values outside of the norm that has left them bereft of purpose and direction.

Modern western society has become increasingly secular, less invested in the narratives and ideals of religion, culminating in a generation that has become demoralized and disinterested in the life principles of the past. This generation has only become further dejected as the fragile economic system that underpinned society culminated in the financial crisis. In a world of instability and obscurity, science and more tangibly nature offer a source of truth and authenticity. Christopher McCandless' ill fated rejection of the human realm in favor of a more primitive, natural existence popularized in the book and later film, 'Into the Wild', epitomizes the attitudes of contempt towards materialism, the rat race of modern living and unrelenting routine. Where do (and where could) these disenchanted go to find themselves?

Architecturally enhanced environments herald the possibility of transforming passive tourist experiences into immersive ones. Augmenting the natural environment by implanting new structures within existing ecosystems will create new platforms for human/environment relationships; providing new forms of human experience and inspiring a greater appreciation of the natural realm. The project seeks to provide a vehicle for the advancement of eco-tourism along the 'experience economy' continuum through the exploration of two key issues: authenticity and immersion. These issues will be explored through the project operating in a speculative future, dramatizing the potential influences of technology and the changing perception of nature on the experience economy.

The project Deus Ex Machina is such an architectural device that acts to transform a unique environment into a meaningful encounter. It does this through the formation of a more intimate and personal experience than the unadulterated environment alone could offer.

Deus Ex Machina acts to manufacture physical layers of information as a means of communication between humans and the environment. It operates to record environmental data and reproduce it by printing the environmental patterns in a material that degrades over time. As the system operates an emergent pattern is produced, actively modeling the volatile flows of energy and material within the local environment. Temporary environmental conditions readily erode, while patterns occurring over larger time frames create more permanent structures within the pattern. The architecture acts to provide a tangible representation of the invisible network of the local ecosystem, enmeshing visitors more deeply into the realities of the site. This deeper representation of environmental systems allows visitors to bear witness to a truer manifestation of the local environment, creating a deeper psychological connection and therefore an enduring memory. The architectural system amplifies the information readily available within the environment, magnifying the connections and interrelationships: exposing visitors to the hidden drama, fragility and complexity of the space.

The deeper immersion of these visitors into the experience of the environment is Deus Ex Machina's primary mode of intensifying human/environment relationships. The architecture operates to provide and expose visitors to far more information than could be garnered from merely occupying the unaugmented site.

Authenticity is a quality inherent within the natural environment itself. The value is derived from the time taken for the site to evolve and stratify into its present state. This authenticity is further warranted in the exposure of the interconnected systems, interdependencies and relationships within the natural ecosystem, embedding the environment in space and time; highlighting its current state as but a fleeting moment in an ever-changing system. It is this appreciation of the legacy beyond the immediately visible that facilitates new opportunities for human experience. However, it also represents a human (synthetic) intrusion within the 'pure' natural condition.

The project readily accepts this paradox. It presents a mutation of the natural, but in such a way that it makes the natural more comprehensible, engaging and memorable to visitors. It is a lens through which human perception can come to see a more complete view of the environment at large. As such Deus Ex Machina offers a deviation from the pristine scenic vistas typically associated with ecotourism. Instead a hybrid condition is created that enables environmental issues to become a key proponent of the site's value. It creates an experience where the binary notions of natural and human can be suspended; offering the space for a paradigm shift whereby travellers can perceive themselves within the larger ecological network. Deus Ex Machina's extrapolation and communication of the intangible facets of the environment act to help people feel involved with the space and to undergo a kind of communion with nature. The focal point of the architectural device occurs where the drama of nature is condensed and collapsed into a single time and space and the climax of the experience materializes. It is an experience that is made more powerful with the constant growth and decay of the system that holds the implicit potential for death, and as such the vulnerability of the system drives the human hunger for an audience with it.

The value of an authentic, embedded environment will only increase as future technologies create the possibility of synthetic experiences. Virtual reality, globalization and artificial environments would allow any imagined experience to be readily manufactured such that authentic experiences of nature increase in value as poor substitutes become increasingly commonplace. In this economy the enduring timelessness juxtaposed with the inherent fragility of natural environments will hold new appeal as experience. The temporality, transitory and interwoven qualities of the natural space create a unique and stimulating experience for visitors, acting to inspire changes in their views and mindset. They are changed by the experience.

The architecture operates as an extension of the ecosystem, acting to manifest and personify the underlying activity occurring just beyond the perception of humans. In this way the environmental network pulls the puppet strings of the architecture and in doing so orchestrates the architecture as the focal point of the wider network. What is created is a modern deity of the environment. An entity that communicates tangibly with humanity. The abstract, shallow and passive experience of the environment is transformed through this infrastructure, as visitors are arrested by the direct and open encounter with nature. Such an experience involves notions of confession and penitence as people seek to find a deeper connection with the environment as an escape from their increasingly sheltered urban lives. It is a space in which the dichotomies of the natural and the human are blurred; a viewpoint from which tourists are

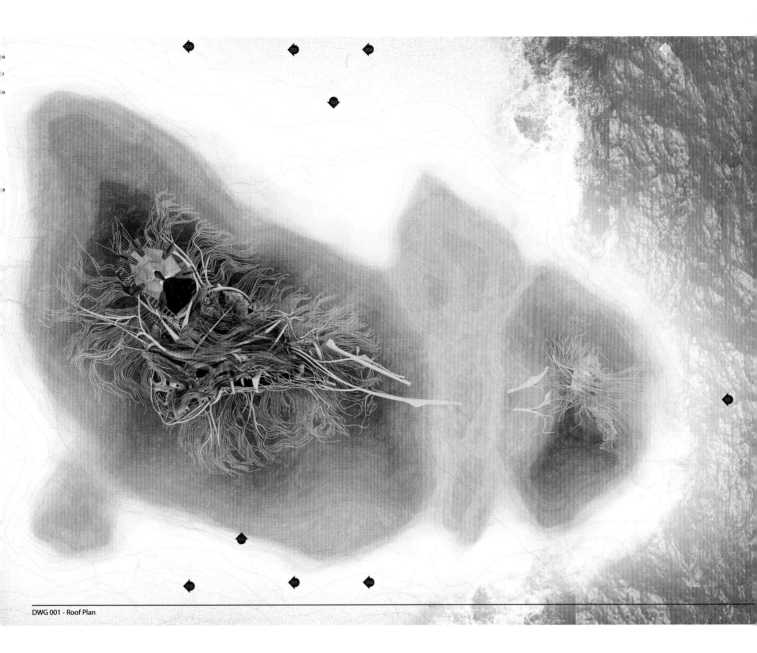

DWG 001 – Roof Plan

able to reflect on their day to day lives 'at home'.

Deus Ex Machina operates as a place of pilgrimage, of indulgence and duty; offering knowledge, self-reflection and appeasement. The experience seeks to reconfigure peoples' attitudes by imparting the ideas of balance and interconnected systems through address-ing the misconception that humans live and operate outside of nature. The tourist is offered not only the mo-mentary experience of the space but is exposed to the possibility of transcending beyond their old lives. Their minds can be opened to the intangible workings of the environment, even if their eyes can only see it through Deus Ex Machina.

The project seeks to drive the notion of enhanced consumerism by offering more than experience: per-sonal growth. Deus Ex Machina provides insight into new possible directions for living, new sets of values, an orientation within the quagmire of open possibility of-fered by modern living. Tourism will no longer be about a holiday dedicated to rejuvenation but rather it seeks to offer the tourist the possibility of being more than when they departed, about growth rather than healing.

ENDNOTES:

1 Krakauer, Jon. *Into the Wild*. New York: Anchor Books, 1997.
2 *Into the Wild*. Dir. Sean Penn. Perf. Emile Hirsch, Maria Gay Harden, William Hurt, Jena Malone. Paramount Vantage, 2008.

F. Català-Roca. *Eduardo Chillida en el Peine del Viento. San Sebastián. 1976* – © Photographic Archive F. Català-Roca – Arxiu Fotogràfic de l'Arxiu Històric del Collegi d'Architectes de Catalunya (AHCOAC). With the collaboration of the Collegi d'Architectes de Catalunya

BETWEEN MEMORY AND INVENTION

AN INTERVIEW WITH NIETO SOBEJANO ARQUITECTOS

by LUIS SACRISTÁN MURGA

Beyond entertainment and culture, or tourism, aspects of the experience economy that have evolved since Pine and Gilmore's seminal 1998 definition, recent concepts focus instead on the role of "place" as experience[1]. Int|AR author Luis Sacristán Murga explores this idea with architects Fuensanta Nieto and Enrique Sobejano, whose projects are exemplary of architectural interventions that contribute to a new and different experience. Beginning with their project for the Museum of San Telmo that is very much a product of "place" in San Sebastián, the designated European Capital of Culture 2016, to key projects of reuse and heritage in Europe, we are offered a unique glimpse into the critical thinking behind their approach to experience and adaptation.

There are few places in the world as San Sebastián, the quintessential picturesque city, where the natural and artificial merge in the absolute. The dialogue with the place generates every action and architectural experience. With a deeply rooted culture and identity, architects and artists have always dealt with its tradition, nature and materials, while incorporating the language of the artistic vanguard.

One of its many poetic corners and possibly the most known place in the city, the Comb of the Wind, was created by sculptor Eduardo Chillida in the middle of the 20th century, on the rocks at one end of the bay. As a prelude to these steel sculptures rusted by the sea, the architect Peña Ganchegui built a platform adapted to the topography through a pixelated landscape of cobbles, creating a public space in the edge between the city, the mountains and the absolute ocean.

"This place is the origin of everything. It is the real author of the work of art (...). My sculpture is the solution to an equation which, instead of numbers, has elements: the sea, the wind, the cliffs, the horizon and the light. The steel forms are mixed with the forces of nature, they converse with them, they are questions and statements."[2]
(Eduardo Chillida, sculptor and poet)

The city appears from the landscape, interlaced with it, in a deep dialogue between epochs and materials, between the natural and the transformed, in which both parts are enhanced to form a new unit, more complete and beautiful.

At the other end of the bay stands the Dominican convent dedicated to San Telmo, saint of sailors, sited at the foot of Mount Urgull and facing the Urumea River. It was built in the mid-sixteenth century, under the patronage of the Secretary of State of Emperor Charles V. This ancient building is a reflection of the city's history, and therefore, it has undergone various transformations and changes of use throughout its lifetime.

After the War of Independence against the French in the nineteenth century, the city of San Sebastián was razed and the convent of San Telmo, left in ruins, was subsequently transformed into military barracks in 1836. Due to its progressive degradation and neglect, the convent was finally purchased by the City Council in 1928, to house the Museum of San Telmo, the oldest museum institution of the Basque Country, founded in 1902.

Following the celebration of its centenary in 2002, the City Council launched a public competition for the extension of the museum. The architectural office Nieto+Sobejano won first prize with a proposal based on the recovery of the original volumes of the convent (chapel, church, cloister and tower), and the extension of the museum through an addition embedded in the topography of Mount Urgull and connected to the historic building in specific places. The work began in 2007 with the rehabilitation project that included the demolition of the volumes added in the twentieth century, in order to recover the original spaces and materials of the historic building. During the work, ancient crypts, paint-

TOP
Plaza del Tenis, 2015

BOTTOM
Old postcard of the aerial view of La Concha beach and historic city

ings and archaeological remains appeared, becoming part of the museum.

The new extension of San Telmo Museum opened in 2011 and became a key element of the recent strategy promoted by the City Council for the recovery of historic urban spaces, which fosters the modernization of the city through the integration of its memory. This philosophy is one of many essential reasons that led to San Sebastián's selection as the European Capital of Culture in 2016.

In addition to providing splendid natural scenery and a refined urban and artistic heritage, the central strategy of the city towards its candidacy for the European Capital of Culture 2016 was to propose a new type of experience economy by way of the concept: "Culture to overcome violence". The Basque Country is currently experiencing a key moment in its recent history leaving behind decades of social conflict and violence, and initiating an era of peace and coexistence. This strategy aims to create spaces for reflection and collective creation, in order to convert European cities into spaces for coexistence. Under a model of respect for Human Rights, it promotes a culture of peace and education in values and in cultural diversity. This innovative approach promotes tourism as an experience that produces personal enrichment to visitors, allowing them to share an experience of coexistence rather than one of mere cultural spectatorship. In addition, the proposal fosters a new kind of creative tourism, linked to the city's cultural professionals and creative industries.

This philosophy could become the paradigm of a new experience economy, one more socially committed and involved in the transformation of society through the cultural and human values of integration.

In this context, Architecture is responsible for hosting the experiences of creation and coexistence, becoming an active element in the process of exchange and social transformation, as in the case of the Museum of San Telmo. Besides representing the spirit of innovation through the interpretation of memory, during 2016 the museum will also become an essential open space for reflection, creation and experimentation for citizens of San Sebastián and those who come from afar.

Museums can serve as elements for social transformation, based on their mission to provide a service to the community. Increasingly, and with the recent social movements where citizens are demanding more empowerment and participation, museums have the opportunity to become spaces for confluence, and therefore must be conceived as "by people and for people"[3].

The memory of a city, its ability to reinvent itself and look into the future without losing its unique and singular personality, reflects the identity of a culture, and that dual concept - local and global - of the human being, which Chillida imagines "as a tree, with the roots in one place, and with the branches open to the world"[4].

Site plan of the San Telmo Museum

CONTEXT AND PLACE AS A TRIGGER OF THE PROJECT

LSM: When intervening in a special context such as San Sebastián, where tradition, nature and the vanguard have always been interlaced, leading to an urban fabric adapted to the landscape, to sculptures and public spaces in the boundaries of the city such as those of Chillida or Peña Ganchegui, and to a contemporary architecture as sensitive and iconic as Rafael Moneo's Kursaal what was your initial approach to the project for the extension of the Museum of San Telmo?

N+S: Clearly those three concepts - tradition, nature and avant-garde- define the circumstances that came together in the project of the Museum of San Telmo: in the boundary between Mount Urgull and the Old Town, in the confluence of nature and city, the horizontal plane and the topographic elevation, land and sea, historic and recent buildings. In that sense the project suggested an architecture conscious of its role in relation to the landscape and history, which does not contradict the will of innovation and transformation. Perhaps for this reason the work was conceived not only to fulfil the needs of the program and its adaptation to the place,

but as a response to the boundary condition. We could say that this is an inhabited building / edge, which responds to the complex relationship between the natural landscape and the cityscape.

LSM: How do you understand the 'spirit of the place', the Genius Loci, in San Sebastián and generally in your projects? Why is the deep understanding of the context so essential for you?

N+S: In San Telmo the new building reacts to a succession of urban spaces: the Plaza de Zuloaga and the connection with Mount Urgull, the Plaza de la Trinidad and the interstitial spaces between the historic building and the extension. We understand the context through the sensations received from the site, but also from the images that subconsciously live in our memory and trigger a series of associations from which the project starts.

LSM: How is it possible to reinterpret a unique context and culture such as the Basque one? How does one produce an identity through architecture? How does architecture create experiences that represent a place and culture?

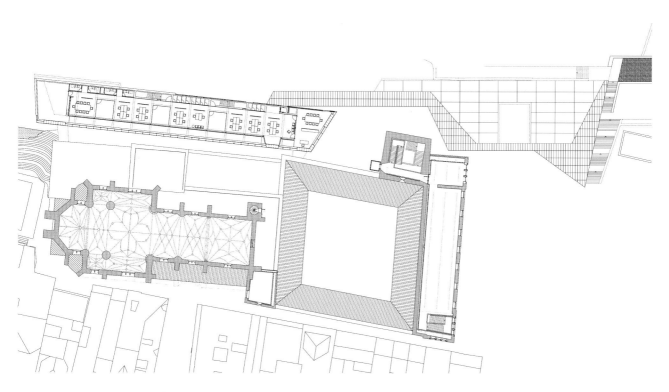

PLANTA +3
0 1   10

Plan at level 3, San Telmo Museum

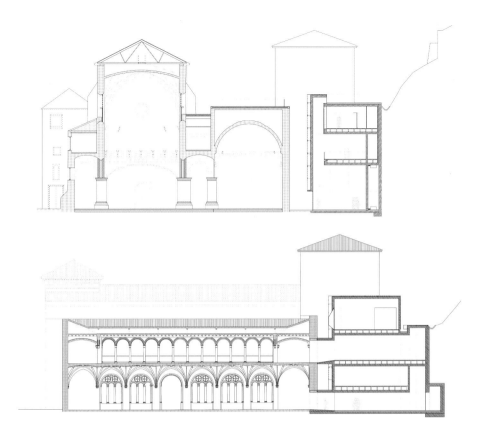

TOP
**Sections cutting through the church, monastery and the extension of the
museum**

BOTTOM
View of plaza at entry to San Telmo Museum

N+S: We do not support generalizations, for example when terms such as "identity", "Basque" architecture or other similar definitions are used. We are interested, on the contrary, in architecture that is able to establish specific connections with a place and a culture through the experience. In this sense, our job is to ultimately uncover the principles or instructions that the context transmits and transform them into new architectural spaces. More than a generic reinterpretation of Basque culture, we understand the extension of San Telmo as a specific intervention, which reacts to the physical conditions and to the memory of a place.

LSM: Our societies have changed from consuming products, then services to recently consuming experiences, in what has been called the Experience Economy. How does this new demand for the consumption of memorable experiences affect architecture?

N+S: The consumption of "memorable" experiences today generates such a wide demand that it paradoxically provokes a rapid oblivion. This happens in almost all areas of culture: blockbuster art exhibitions and performances as well as literary best sellers. Architecture however, due to its physical reality, constructive and spatial, has different characteristics. Despite suffering a constant overexposure in the media, the direct experience of a building requires time and attention, making it more durable. The so-called Experience Economy has put into its service certain institutions, such as museums, but as opposed to the mere consumption of images, the sensory and spatial experience is the only thing that makes architecture comprehensible.

LSM: Is there a culture of spectacle versus a culture of authenticity in architecture? Is there a division between a stream of global projection of more decontextualized architecture and another one more local and rooted to the context?

N+S: We are conscious that architecture should be experienced directly through the senses. But this phenomenological experience is much more limited than the one which comes through printed or audiovisual media, or through the network. How many of the buildings that are criticized, admired or rejected are a result of a live experience? Facing the global society and its need to consume images, architecture has an advantage over other arts and disciplines: building takes time, it is not immediate, the experience of a building involves travelling, visiting, observing and perceiving with the senses, something that the culture of entertainment cannot substitute with the immediate image. There is no division between decontextualized architecture and "authentic" architecture, since any architectural work is likely to be experienced. But there is a different attitude towards the project: some works are conceived by their authors with a purely iconic will, with the essential purpose of the image, while a very different attitude is the one that is originated in the spatial, material and cultural qualities, which link a building to a place.

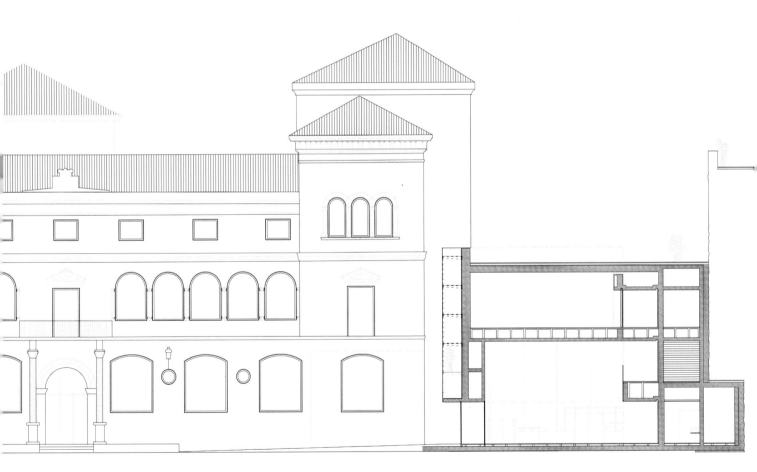

Section through the extension of San Telmo Museum

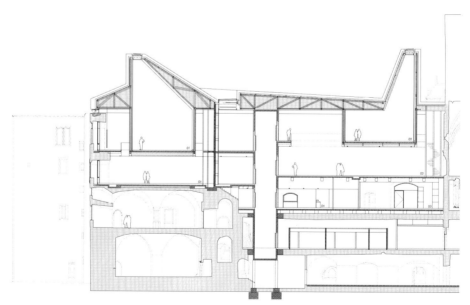

TOP
New roof volumes, Moritzburg Museum

BOTTOM
Section through the galleries, Moritzburg Museum

PUBLIC SPACE, MATERIALS AND MEMORY

LSM: In what way do you think a city like San Sebastián will be affected by being the European Capital of Culture 2016? How important are these events for a city and for its people?

N+S: These events represent the opportunity to carry out works and cultural investments that otherwise would not be launched, or would have been delayed indefinitely in time. In that sense they are always positive. Our project for San Telmo was, however, prior to the proposed capital, and it was actually a result of a demand for renovation that had existed for many years.

LSM: The public spaces of San Sebastián are one of its wonderful urban experiences. Why should the creation of public space be always present in the background of architectural projects? What is the importance of having a good network of public spaces in a city?

N+S: Architecture, even in programs for private use, always has a public dimension and responsibility towards the urban space or the landscape. With institutional projects, such as a museum, the demand is even bigger. Therefore it is not inaccurate to think that the urban dimension of a building transcends the interior. The history of San Telmo confirms it; the successive uses have been changing: convent, church, military barracks or municipal museum, while its presence in the city and the public spaces that it generates have remained over time.

Gallery at Moritzburg Museum showing new interventions within the castle walls

LSM: For the construction of the Plaza de la Trinidad, which borders the Museum of San Telmo on its western part, Peña Ganchegui, in the 60's, reused old cobblestones, found in the city council's storage, due to the limitations of the project budget. But by using these old materials with a modern language, he established a unique material relationship with the context, giving new meaning to elements that had lost their significance. Are materials an essential element of integration with the context and a dialogue between epochs? What do you value most when you define the materials in your projects?

N+S: The materials and construction systems that we use in our works are the result of the architectural idea that generates each project: they supplement it and they are its formal support. In other words, the material expression of a building should reflect its relationship with the city, the landscape or the memory of a place. The extension of the Moritzburg Museum was conceived as a folded metal deck that merges with the usually cloudy skies of that place. In the Center for Contemporary Art in Córdoba, prefabricated panels of GCR define a topography whose geometry evokes the ornamentation of the Islamic architecture. In San Telmo, the façade of perforated aluminum panels allows the growth of mosses and lichens in certain places, alluding to the rock and vegetation of Mount Urgull.

LSM: The experience of space varies depending on its materials as they produce different perceptions, smells, tactile sensations, textures, meanings... How do you understand the relationships between different materials? In the reuse and adaptation of heritage, are there materials that inherently hold an element of greater authenticity?

N+S: When speaking about appropriate materials for intervention in architectonic heritage, we would have to distinguish between works of renovation and works of extension. In the renovation or rehabilitation of an historic monument, it is the process itself that leads us to understand the problem through the action of developing and constructing it. We often use similar materials to those of the original building, like stone, stucco, wood, ceramic and copper. When it comes to a new building or an extension our approach is based on a dialogue with the existing materials. For example, in Madinat al-Zahra, we use white concrete and rusted steel, contemporary materials that "talk" with the stucco and the ceramic of the ancient Hispanic Moorish city. In San Sebastián, the lattice panels of aluminum transform the project in an intervention that links architecture to public art.

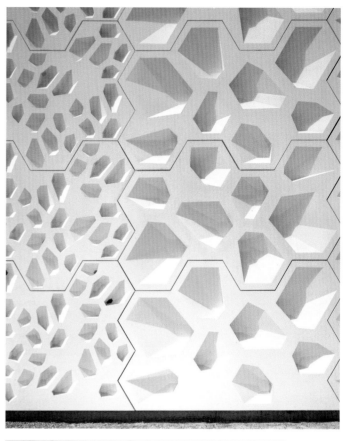

LSM: In your projects, the use of an outer skin with a special treatment that gives a unique texture to each building is recurrent: in the extension of the Museum of San Telmo, it has much to do with the mimesis with the natural context, in the Congress Center of Mérida, with establishing a more detailed scale, and in the Contemporary Art Centre of Córdoba with integrating the digital world into the facade. Is the exterior facade a reinterpreted mirror of the context in your projects? Which is the relationship that you look for between these two scales of distance and proximity?

N+S: Clearly the works of Mérida, San Telmo and the Art Center in Córdoba are part of a similar concept for the design of the outer skin. In the three cases the expressive value of the material modulates the scale and relationship with the physical environment. In the three projects it comes to collaborations undertaken with contemporary artists in the definition of a texture developed specifically for each occasion: Esther Pizarro in the bas-relief of the city of Mérida, Ferrán and Otero in the green facade of Mount Urgull, and Realities:united in the digital screen in Córdoba. The three projects reflect our interest in the fringe or the limit of where the visual arts, architecture and urban space converge.

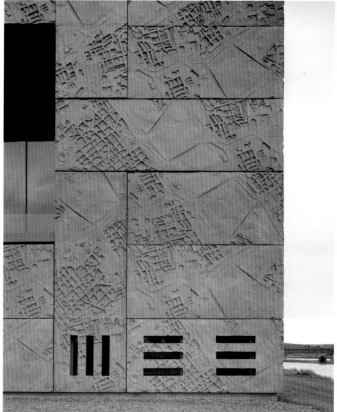

TOP
Facade, Center for Contemporary Art, Córdoba
BOTTOM
Facade, Congress Center, Mérida

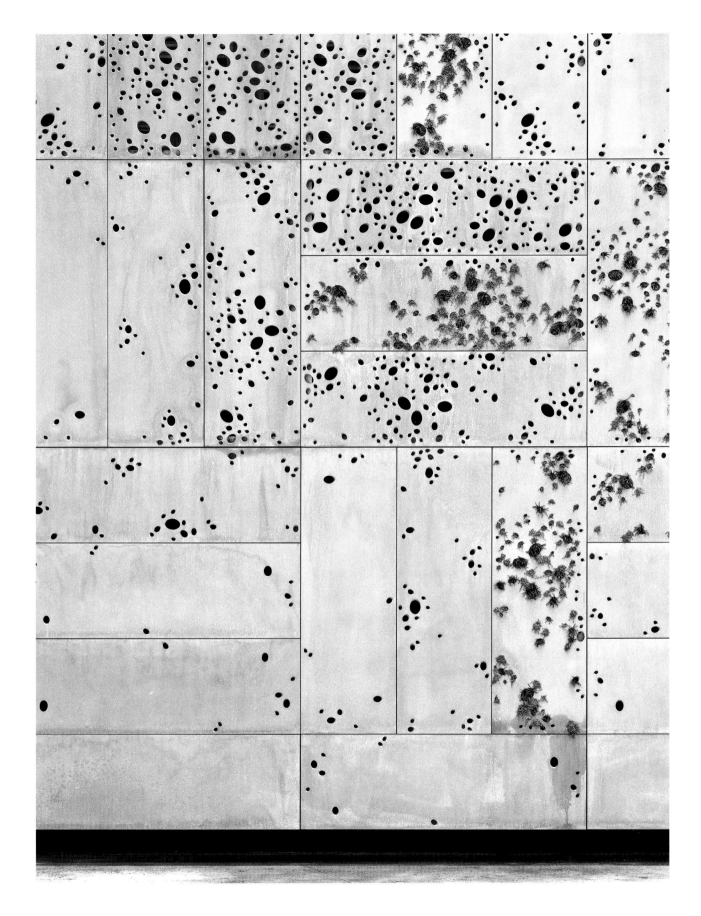

Facade of San Telmo Museum, San Sebastián

Congress Center, Mérida

REUSE AND ADAPTATION OF CULTURAL HERITAGE

LSM: In addition to the extension of the Museum of San Telmo, you have many other projects related to the Adaptive Reuse of cultural heritage, including the Museum of Madinat Al-Zahra in Córdoba, the Castillo de la Luz in Las Palmas, and the art galleries Kastner & Ohler in Graz. What about the Adaptive Reuse of heritage is of particular interest to you?

N+S: We are interested in heritage intervention for its requirement of the taking of a stand in the transformation of architecture in space and time. The rehabilitation of works of the past forces us to read a building as the sum of different juxtaposed texts, in which the new intervention is another chapter of its long history. This also reflects a clear difference between architecture and other artistic disciplines. It is not admitted, in principle, that a pictorial, sculptural, musical, cinematic or literary work of art could be modified by another author, but it has always been assumed that buildings can change use or be extended and transformed by other architects. We could say that rehabilitation and intervention in existing buildings are precisely the condition that distinguishes architecture from other arts.

LSM: Should architecture have 'roots'? How is it possible to dialogue with Time? How do memory and the past, the present and innovation come together?

N+S: We have referred several times to our work as a dialogue between memory and invention. The process by which an abstract idea becomes a concrete result is constantly nourished by latent images in our memory. Therein probably lies the profound relationship of architecture with time.

View of Joanneumsviertel in historic Graz

Through the glass insertions at the Joanneumsviertel, Graz

LSM: What is the power of architecture and adaptive reuse that transforms consciousness, transmits values, and generates experiences of a place through its history?

N+S: Intervening in heritage involves the inquiry of the meaning of the present and the registration of the past. Any new intervention is, on one hand temporary, and on the other a reflection of its historical reality. In a work of adaptive reuse it is not easy to determine authorship. It is not already the work of a single architect, but of several throughout its history, which transmits a social and collective experience and value.

LSM: What is the boundary between what to and what not to keep in cities? Do you agree with Rem Koolhaas, when he says that 'preservation is overtaking us'?

N+S: We have passed from the initial disinterest of Modern architecture for heritage – where historic landmarks were considered as isolated facts, while other buildings inherited from the past should simply be substituted - to the current attitude, especially European, which protects, sometimes in excess, any building of the past. Naturally, we do not agree with these extreme options, but with a balance whose limit lies in the architectural quality of each intervention itself.

LSM: What is your experience for intervening in UNESCO protected historical environments as in your project in Graz? What should the balance be between construction and preservation in an historical context, so that it does not become a mere tourist attraction, as is the historic center of Venice, where the inhabitants have moved to the suburbs and only touristic services such as shops and hotels remain in the city center?

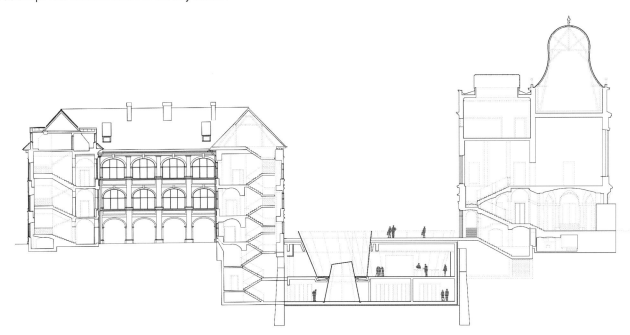

Section through the Joanneumsviertel, Graz

Entrance and Addition, Castillo de la Luz, Las Palmas

N+S: In Graz, the problem is common to many historical cities protected by UNESCO.

The alternative is often raised in these opposing terms: all new buildings in the old town should be carried out by imitating the forms and materials of an era that is considered the most appropriate to their history and any contemporary intervention would imply the destruction of their identity. Of course we do not agree with this dichotomy.

We understand that the city must remain active and alive so we believe that new interventions require a careful balance between memory of the place, its scale and contemporary needs. Fortunately, in Graz our project was interpreted this way.

LSM: Where is Adaptive Reuse moving towards? What is the future of the architecture of memory?

N+S: Adaptive reuse and the transformation of buildings will not be limited in the future only to those considered of historical value because, in our opinion, all architecture - of new creation or of rehabilitation - is always the result of an interpretation of memory.

Nieto Sobejano Arquitectos was founded in 1985 by Fuensanta Nieto and Enrique Sobejano and has offices in Madrid and, since 2007, in Berlin. Along with being widely published in international magazines and books, the firm's work has been exhibited at the Biennale di Venezia in 2000, 2002, 2006, and 2012; at the Museum of Modern Art (MoMA), New York, in 2006, at the Kunsthaus in Graz in 2008 and at the MAST Foundation in Bologna, Italy in 2014. They are the recipients of the 2008 National Prize for Restoration from the Spanish Ministry of Culture and the 2010 Nike Prize issued by the Bund Deutscher Architekten (BDA), as well as the Aga Khan Award for Architecture (2010), the Piranesi Prix de Rome (2011), the European Museum of the Year Award (2012), the Hannes Meyer Prize (2012), Honorary Fellow of AIA (2015) and the Alvar Aalto Medal in 2015. Their major works include the Madinat al-Zahra Museum, the Moritzburg Museum, the San Telmo Museum, the Joanneum extension in Graz, and the Contemporary Art Centre in Córdoba. Nieto Sobejano Arquitectos currently have projects in Germany, Spain, Austria, Estonia and Morocco.

Addition at Castillo de la Luz, Las Palmas

PROJECT CREDITS, INFORMATION AND BIBLIOGRAPHIES

EDITORIAL

Image sources from left to right:
Figure 01, 02_Courtesy of Liliane Wong; Figure 03 http://upload.wikimedia.org/wikipedia/commons/d/d8/Expo_SACRED_Venice_ai_weiwei_1.JPG, By Abxbay (Own work) [CC BY-SA 3.0 (http://creativecommons.org/licenses/by-sa/3.0)], via Wikimedia Commons; Figure 04_"Tate.modern.weather.project" by Michael Reeve - Photograph taken by Michael Reeve, 21 November 2003. Licensed under CC BY-SA 3.0 via Wikimedia Commons - http://commons.wikimedia.org/wiki/File:Tate.modern.weather.project.jpg#/media/File:Tate.modern.weather.project.jpg; Figure 05_Courtesy of Marianna Bender; Figure 06_Jesús Uriarte.

BIBLIOGRAPHY

_ http://www.lelaboratoire.org/en/products.php
_ "The Unilever Series: Olafur Eliasson: The Weather Project," http://www.tate.org.uk
_ Tabucchi, Antonio. (translated by Alistair McEwan) It's Getting Later All the Time, New Directions Books, Antonella Antonelli Letteria, SRI, Milan, 2001.
_ Chillida, Eduardo. (translated by Luis Sacristán Murga),"Speech in the Doctorate Honoris Causa Ceremony," University of Alicante, 1996.

NEW PASTS, OLD EXPERIENCES

Project name_Cairo Agriculture Museum in Dokki, Cairo, Egypt; Key architects_"Egyptian Government Architects"; Owner_Princess Fatima Ismail; Museum opened_1938, Restoration_1996, Expansion_2002; Image sources_Figure 01_Courtesy of Xenia Nikolskaya from the series, DUST: Egypt's Forgotten Architecture; Figure 02_Sourced by the author from Getty Images; Figure 03_Licensed under the Attribution-NonCommercial-ShareAlike 2.0 license. https://www.flickr.com/photos/naturewise/5408059712/in/photostream/; Figure 04_Courtesy Xenia Nikolskaya; Figure 05_Licensed under the Attribution-NonCommercial-ShareAlike 2.0 license. https://www.flickr.com/photos/naturewise/5407447147/

BIBLIOGRAPHY

- Adorno, Theodor W. The Language of Authenticity, translated by Knut Tarnowski and Frederic Will (Evanston: Northwestern University Press, 1973).
- Koolhaas, Rem. "Preservation is Overtaking Us," Future Anterior, Vol.1, No. 2, Fall 2004.
- Coleman, Anthony. Millenium, (Transworld Publishers, 1999).
- Gershoni, Israel and Jankowski, James P. Redefining the Egyptian Nation, 1930-1945 (Cambridge: Cambridge University Press, 1995).
- Samih, Mai "The Grassroots on Display," Al-Ahram Weekly, Issue No. 1129, January 3, 2013 (accessed September 23, 2014).
- Hassan, Fayza. "The Forgotten Museums of Egypt," Museum: Heritage Landscape of Egypt, No. 225-226, Vol LVII, 2005 (accessed September 23, 2014).

APPROXIMATIONS TO A WORKING SPACE

Project name_El Museo de Los Sures, New York, New York, USA; Image sources_Courtesy of Laura F. Gibellini.

BIBLIOGRAPHY

-Bauman, Zygmunt. Liquid Modernity. Cambridge, UK; Malden, MA: Polity Press, 2000.
-Derrida, Jacques. Psyche: Inventions of the Other, vol. 1. California: Standford University Press, 2007.
-England, Jeremy L. "Statistical physics of self-replication". AIP The Journal of Chemical Physics 139, 121923 (2013): 1-8. Accessed August 10, 2014. doi: 10.1063/1.4818538.
-Latour, Bruno. "Air". In Sensorium: Embodied Experience, Technology and Contemporary Art, edited by Caroline A. Jones, 104 - 107. Cambridge, MA: MIT Press, 2006.
-Sloterdijk, Peter. Sphären III. Schäume. Frankfurt: Suhrkamp, 2004.
-Sloterdijk, Peter. "Atmospheric Politics". In Making Things Public. Atmospheres of Democracy, edited by Bruno Latour and Peter Weibel, 944 – 951. Cambridge, MA: MIT Press, 2005.
-Steinberg, Philip E. "Of other seas: metaphors and materialities in maritime regions", Atlantic Studies, 10:2, (2013): 156 –169. Accessed July 27, 2014. Doi:10.1080/14788810.2013.785192

A VISUAL HISTORY OF DINING

Image sources_Opening figure_Dinner in White, Paris. "It happens once a year in early summer: By the hundreds and thousands, on a date determined city-by-city, people around the world, dressed in white, meet at a previously-agreed "forbidden" spot — generally a beautiful, central public location in the heart of a city – to share a gourmet dinner with friends. They bring tables, chairs, tablecloths, candelabra, china, silver and an elaborate meal." Forbes Magazine, Cecilia Rodriquez. July 11th, 2014. Image licensed under the Creative Commons Attribution 2.0 Generic license. https://www.flickr.com/photos/parisharing/9038215778/sizes/l; Figures listed in general clockwise from top right: Figure 01_Permission is granted to copy, distribute, and/or modify this document under the terms of the GNU Free Documentation License, Version 1.2 or any later version published by the Free Software Foundation; with no Invariant Sections, no Front-Cover Texts, and no Back-Cover Texts. Licensed under the Creative Commons Attribution-Share Alike 3.0 Unported license. http://en.wikipedia.org/wiki/Printing_press; Figure 02_This image (or other media file) is in the public domain because its copyright has expired. http://commons.wikimedia.org/wiki/File:M-A-Careme.jpg; Figure 03_This image is in the public domain because its copyright has expired. http://commons.wikimedia.org/wiki/File:Luxury_on_wheels.jpg; Figure 04_This file is licensed under the Creative Commons Attribution-Share Alike 3.0 Unported license. http://commons.wikimedia.org/wiki/File:H%C3%B4tel_de_Crozat.jpg; Figure 05_ This media file is in the public domain in the United States. This applies to the U.S. works where the copyright has expired, often because its first publication occurred prior to January 1, 1923. http://commons.wikimedia.org/wiki/File:Delmonicos.jpg; Figure 06_Permission is granted to copy, distribute and/or modify this document under the terms of the GNU Free Documentation License, Version 1.2 or any later version published by the Free Software Foundation; with no Invariant Sections, no Front-Cover Texts, and no Back-Cover Texts. http://commons.wikimedia.org/wiki/File:P1170414_Paris_VI_quai_des_Grands-Augustins_Laperouse_rwk.jpg; Figure 07_This image is in the public domain because its copyright has expired. http://en.wikipedia.org/wiki/Coffeehouse#/media/File:ParisCafeDiscussion.png; Figure 08_ This image is available from the United States Library of Congress's Prints and Photographs division under the digital ID ppprs.00626 http://commons.wikimedia.org/wiki/File:First_flight2.jpg; Figure 09_Licensed under the Creative Commons Attribution 3.0 United States (cc by 3.0 us) license. http://www.famouswiki.com/people/41308/fernand-point.html; Figure 10_This file is licensed under the Creative Commons Attribution-Share Alike 3.0 Unported license. http://commons.wikimedia.org/wiki/File:Guide_michelin_1929_couverture-edit.png; Figure 11_This image or file is a work of the United States Department of Commerce employee, taken or made as a part of the person's official duties. As a work of the U.S. federal government, the image is in the public domain. http://commons.wikimedia.org/wiki/File:Interstate_Highway_plan_September_1955.jpg; Figure 12_This image is a work of a U.S. Army soldier or employee, taken or made as part of that person's official duties. As a work of the U.S. federal government, this image is in the public domain. http://commons.wikimedia.org/wiki/File:American_military_personnel_gather_in_Paris_to_celebrate_the_Japanese_surrender.jpg; Figure 13_This file is licensed under the Creative Commons Attribution 3.0 Unported license. http://commons.wikimedia.org/

wiki/File:Douglas_DC-6A_PH-TGA_KLM_LAP_10.10.53_edited-2.jpg; Figure 14_Permission is granted to copy, distribute and/or modify this document under the terms of the GNU Free Documentation License, Version 1.2 or any later version published by the Free Software Foundation; with no Invariant Sections, no Front-Cover, and no Back-Cover Texts. http://commons.wikimedia.org/wiki/File:Jacques_Lameloise,_escab%C3%A8che_d%27%C3%A9crevisses_sur_gaspacho_d%27asperge_et_cresson.jpg; Figure 15_Permission is granted to copy, distribute and/or modify this document under the terms of the GNU Free Documentation License, Version 1.2 or any later version published by the Free Software Foundation; with no Invariant Sections, no Front-Cover Texts, and no Back-Cover Texts. http://commons.wikimedia.org/wiki/File:FedEx_Express_truck.jpg; Figure 16_Image is licensed under the Attribution-Non Commercial-Share Alike 2.0 Generic license. https://www.flickr.com/photos/cronicasdesdelomejordelagastronomia/5166924196/; Figure 17_This is a logo of an organization, item, or event, and is protected by copyright. It is believed that the use of low-resolution images on the English-language Wikipedia, hosted on servers in the United States by the non-profit Wikimedia Foundation, of logos for certain uses involving identification and critical commentary may qualify as fair use under United States copyright law. Any other use of this image, on Wikipedia or elsewhere, may be copyright infringement. http://en.wikipedia.org/wiki/File:Logo_PSOE_2013.png; Figure 18_This file is licensed under the Creative Commons Attribution 2.0 Generic license http://commons.wikimedia.org/wiki/File:Chef_Thomas_Keller_(4202807186).jpg; Figure 19_This image is licensed under the Creative Commons Attribution 2.0 Generic license. http://commons.wikimedia.org/wiki/File:Alice_Waters_at_Viader_Vinyards,_Napa.jpg; Figure 20_This photograph is part of a collection donated to the Library of Congress. Per the deed of gift, U.S. News & World Report dedicated to the public all rights it held for the photographs in this collection upon its donation to the Library. Thus, there are no known restrictions on the usage of this photograph. http://commons.wikimedia.org/wiki/File:NY_stock_exchange_traders_floor_LC-U9-10548-6.jpg; Figure 21_This file is licensed under the Creative Commons Attribution-Share Alike 3.0 Unported license. http://commons.wikimedia.org/wiki/File:Ren%C3%A9_Redzepi_en_la_cena_de_las_14_estrellas_Michel%C3%ADn_del_restaurante_Zaldiar%C3%A1n.jpg; Figure 22_This file is licensed under the Creative Commons Attribution 2.0 Generic license. http://commons.wikimedia.org/wiki/File:Noma_entrance.jpghttp://commons.wikimedia.org/wiki/File:Noma_entrance.jpg; Figure 23_This file is licensed under the Creative Commons Attribution-Share Alike 3.0 Unported license. http://commons.wikimedia.org/wiki/File:Steve_Jobs_Headshot_2010-CROP.jpg; Figure 24_This file is licensed under the Creative Commons Attribution Alike 2.0 Generic license. http://en.wikipedia.org/wiki/Fast_food_worker_strikes#/media/File:July_29,_2013_Protestor.jpg; Figure 25_This work was created by Guillaume Paumier. With proper credit as follows, you are free to use the work for any purpose. https://guillaumepaumier.com/ Guillaume Paumier, CC-BY. http://commons.wikimedia.org/wiki/File:Mark_Zuckerberg_at_the_37th_G8_Summit_in_Deauville_018_v1.jpg; Figure 26_This image only consists of simple geometric shapes and/or text. It does not meet the threshold of originality needed for copyright protection, and is therefore in the public domain. Although it is free of copyright restrictions, this image may still be subject to other restrictions. http://commons.wikimedia.org/wiki/File:Logo_Google_2013_Official.svg; Figure 27_This file is licensed under the Creative Commons Attibution-Share Alike 3.0 Unported license. http://commons.wikimedia.org/wiki/File:Starbucks_stores_graph.png

THE CHANGING ROLES

Project 01 name_Shopping Stadsfeestzaal, Antwerp, Belgium; Designers_Exners Tegnestue; Owner_Ferre Verbaenen, Ro Berteloot; Restoration & Execution_Ro Berteloot; Contractor_Arcade nv; Photographer_Muti Development Belgium nv; Project Completed_2007; Website of design firm_www.abvplusarchitecten.be; Project 02_Bookstore Dominicanen, Maastricht, (NL); Design

Firm_Merkx+Girod; Project Team_Evelyne Merkx, Patrice Giord, Bert de Munnik, Abbie Steinhauser, Josje Kuiper, Pim Houben, Ramon Wijsman, Ruben Bu; Photographer_Roos Aldershoff; Project completed_2007; Website of design firm_merkx-girod.nl/; Project 03_De Nieuwe Eiffel, Maastricht, (NL); Design firm_Phidias Community Innovation; Website of design firm_www.phidias.pro; Image sources_Figure 01_Courtesy of Markus Berger; Figure 02_Bookshop Dominicanen Maastricht (NL), picture by Bert Kaufmann retrieved from http://commons.wikimedia.org/wiki/File:Not_just_bibles_in_this_church_..._(EXPLORE)_(5679870318).jpg?uselang=nl, accessed September 25, 2014; Figure_03 Bookshop Dominicanen Maastricht (NL), picture retrieved from http://www.vvvmaastricht.nl/boekhandel-dominicanen.html, accessed September 25, 2014; Figure 04_ Pop-Up store Comme des Garçons Warsaw (PL), picture retrieved from http://blogretailrefugees.files.wordpress.com/2008/09/comme-garcons-guerilla-store-warsaw-1.jpg, accessed September 25, 2014; Figure 05_niewe eiffel_Sphinx_Eifel_2e.etage. Licensed under the Creative Commons Attribution-Share Alike 3.0 Unported license. http://nl.wikipedia.org/wiki/Eiffelgebouw#/media/File:Sphinx_Eifel_2e_etage.JPG; Figure 06_niewe eiffel_Sphinx_fabriek_Brusselsestraat_2. Licensed under the Creative Commons Atribution-Share Alike 3.0 Unported, 2.5 Generic, 2.0 Generic and 1.0 Generic license. http://commons.wikimedia.org/wiki/File:Sphinx_fabriek_Brusselsestraat_2.JPG

BIBLIOGRAPHY

-Petermans, Ann. "Retail Design in the Experience Economy: Conceptualizing and 'Measuring' Customer Experiences in Retail Environments." PhD diss., Hasselt University, 2012.
-Cha, T., C. Chung, J. Gunter, D. Herman, H. Hosoya, S. Leong, K. Matsushita, J. McMorrough, J. Palop-Casado, M. Schaefer, T Vinh, S. Weiss, and L. Wyman. "Shopping. Harvard Project on the city." In *Mutations. Harvard Project on the city 1*, edited by R. Koolhaas, S. Boeri, S. Kwinter, N. Tazi, and H. Obrist. Köln: Taschen, 2001.
-Pine, Joseph B., and James H. Gilmore. *The Experience Economy - Work is theatre and every business a stage*. Boston: Harvard Business School Press, 1999.
-Petermans, Ann, and Koenraad Van Cleempoel. "Designing a retail store environment for the mature market: a European perspective." *Journal of Interior Design* 35(2) (2010): 21-36. DOI: 10.1111/j.1939-1668.2009.01036.x.
-Plevoets, Bie. "Retail-Reuse: an interior view on adaptive reuse of buildings." PhD diss., Hasselt University, 2014.
-Plevoets, Bie, Ann Petermans, and Koenraad Van Cleempoel. "(Re)using historic buildings as a retail differentiation strategy." In *Heritage 2012*, edited by R. Amoêda, S. Lira, and C. Pinheiro. Porto: Green Lines Institute, 2012.
-Plevoets, Bie, and Koenraad Van Cleempoel. "Creating sustainable retail interiors through reuse of historic buildings." *Interiors: design, architecture, culture* 3(3) (2012): 271-293. DOI: http://dx.doi.org/10.2752/204191212X13470263747031.
-Klingmann, Anna. *Brandscapes. Architecture in the experience economy*. Cambridge: The MIT Press, 2007.
-Shopping Stadsfeestzaal. "Our aim". Accessed September 24, 2014. http://stadsfeestzaal.com/en/our-aim/.
-Lindgreen, Adam and Michael B. Beverland. "Hush, it's a secret: how trappist breweries create and maintain images of authenticity using customer experiences." In *Memorable customer experiences. A research anthology*, edited by Adam Lindgreen, Joëlle Vanhamme, and Michael B. Beverland. Burlington: Gower Publishing Company, 2009.
-Plevoets, Bie, Ann Petermans, and Koenraad Van Cleempoel. "Developing a theoretical framework for understanding (staged) authentic retail settings in relation to the current experience economy." Paper presented at Design Research Society Conference, Montreal, Canada, July 7-9, 2010.
-Trendwatching. "Pop-up Retail." Last modified in 2004. Accessed November 16, 2011. http:// trendwatching.com/trends/POP-UP_RETAIL.htm () ; Dowdy, C. *One-off Independent Retail Design*. London: Laurence King Publishing, 2008 ; Guerrilla-store. "Guer-

rilla Marketing – a Trend Made In Japan." Last modified in 2009. Accessed November 17, 2011. http://www.guerrilla-store.com/ ().
-Van Cleempoel, Koenraad. "The Relationship between Contemporary Art and Retail Design." Paper presented at Places and Themes of Interior, Milan, October 1–3, 2008.
-Stelwagen, H., Bloemen, P., Petit, J., de Waal Malefijt, C., Pedroli, M., and J.Kemerink. "De Nieuwe Eiffel. Haalbaarheidstudie Eiffel gebouw Maastricht",2013.

POSTINDUSTRIAL SPECTACLE

Project name_SoMA: The simulator of Mechanized Authenticity, Bethlehem, Pennsylvania, USA; Design firm_Syracuse University Thesis Project; Owner_The City of Bethlehem, PA; Photographer_Jean-Francois Bedard & Edward Sichta; Website of design firm_cargocollective.com/pjr; Image sources_Figure 1-4,6 Author, "SoMA": The Simulator of Mechanized Authenticity." (B.Arch Thesis, Syracuse, University, 2013); available from http://cargocollective. com/pjr/undergradute-architecture-thesis; Figure 5 – Permissions and full resolution courtesy of the photographer, Jeffrey Totaro.

BIBLIOGRAPHY

n/a

CATHEDRALS OF CONSUMERISM

Image source_All images courtesy of the author, Sylvia Leydecker.

BIBLIOGRAPHY

-Leydecker, Sylvia. *Corporate Interiors*, avedition, Stuttgart, 2014.

MORE OF SOMETHING ELSE

Image sources_Figure 01_ Hugo Gernsback_1963_TV Glasses. Licensed under the Attribution-Non Commerical-Share Alike 2.0 creative commons license. https://www.flickr.com/photos/x-ray_delta_one/4265173624; Figure 02_This image is in the public domain because the copyright has expired. http://commons.wikimedia.org/wiki/File:Palais_Garnier_transverse_section_at_the_auditorium_and_pavilions_-_Beauvert_1996_p106. jpg; Figure 03_Image released by the copyright holder into the public domain. Use of this work for any purpose, without conditions, unless such conditions are required by law, is granted. http://en.wikipedia.org/wiki/File:Redstone_in_Grand_Central. jpg; Figure 04_Ceiling of the Nave at St. Ignatius of Loyola. This file is licensed under the Creative Commons Attribution-Share Alike 2.0 Generic license. http://en.wikipedia.org/wiki/Andrea_Pozzo; Figure 5-7_ *Locomotion*, Tel Aviv Museum of Art Opening Ceremony Video Mapping Projection. Tali Yacobi Productions, 2011. http:// vimeo.com/49434733; Figure 8-9_ John Ensor Parker, Blueprints & Perspectives. 2013. Screenshot from https://www.youtube.com/ watch?v=52SK_KLa6ss

BIBLIOGRAPHY

-*Locomotion*, Tel Aviv Museum of Art Opening Ceremony Video Mapping Projection. Tali Yacobi Productions, 2011. http://vimeo. com/49434733
- Parker, John Ensor. *Blueprints & Perspectives*. 2013. https://www. youtube.com/watch?v=52SK_KLa6ss
- Venturi, Robert, Scott Brown, Denise and Izenour, Steven. *Learning from Las Vegas*. MIT Press, 1977.

ALTERNATE HOSPITALITY

Project name_25 Hours Hotel Bikini, Berlin, Germany; Design firm_Studio Aisslinger; Key architects_Werner Aisslinger, Janis Nachtigall, Tina Bunyaprasit, Dirk Borchering; Owner_25hours; Contractor_Electricity: B+M Elektrobau GmbH ung Hafemeister Plan GmbH; TGA Firma Ga-Tec Gebäude und Anlagentechnik GmbH; Interior construction: Firma Hagenauer GmbH; Facade: Firma Dobler Metallbau Werksätten GmbH; Photographer_Flur Gross; Project Completed_2013; Website of design firm_www. aisslinger.de; Image sources_Figure 01_ *Public Camping*, Public Design Festival by Esterni, 2011. Image by Delfino Legnani; Figure 02_*Sharing dinner* by Marije Vogelzang, Tokyo, 2008. Image by

Kenji Masunaga; Figure 03_ Studio Aisslinger, *25 hours Hotel Bikini*, Berlin, 2013. Image courtesy of the author, Tiziano A. Rinella; Figure 04-05_*EXA structure*, YES WE CAMP!, Marseille European Capital of Culture 2013. Image by Sébastien Normand; Figure 06_*Public* Camping, Public Design Festival by Esterni, 2011. Image by Guglielmo Trupia.

BIBLIOGRAPHY

- Collina, L. "Expo 2015. Un laboratorio ambientale", in *Milano. Laboratorio del moderno*, Innesti/grafting, catalogo della 14° Mostra Internazionale di Architettura, Biennale di Venezia, vol.2, Marsilio, 2014.
-For further understanding, Aglieri Rinella, T. *Food Experience, design e architettura di interni*, Postmediabooks, Milan, 2014.
- Pine, B.J. and Gilmore, J.H. op.cit.
- Aglieri Rinella, T. *Hotel Design*, Marsilio, Venice, 2011.
-"Interview with Werner Aisslinger", in *Ottagono* n. 270, May 2014.
- Scullica, F. "Online hospitality: an Italian excellence: new scenarios", in *Ottagono* n. 270, May 2014.
-http://www.bedsharing.org
- Algani, E. "Pop-up hospitality for events", in *Ottagono* n. 270, May 2014.
-The five design principles are: theme the experience, harmonize impressions with positive cues, eliminate negative cues, mix in memorabilia and engage the five senses. Cf. Pine, B.J. and Gilmore, J.H. op.cit.

BIKINI BERLIN

Project name_Revitalisation Bikini Berlin, Berlin, Germany; Name of design firm_Hild und K Berlin; Key architects_BT B (Zoopalast), Philip Argyrakis BT C (Bikinihaus), Ulrike Muckermann, Jan Schneidewind, Susanne Welcker; BT D (Kleines Hochhaus) und BT E (Parkhaus), Julia Otte; Designers_Masterplan: SAQ Architects (B); Owner_Bayerische Hausbau GmbH & CoKG; Structural Engineer_WTM Engineers GmbH, GuD Planungsgesellschaft für Ingenieurbau mbH; Photographer_Franz Brük, Berlin; Website of design firm_www.hildundk.de
Image sources_http://www.hildundk.de/bildarchiv-new/?level_1=Bildarchiv&level_2=Bauen%20im%20 Bestand&level_3=Revitalisierung%20Bikini%20Berlin

BIBLIOGRAPHY

-https://www.bikiniberlin.de/en/bikini_berlin/what_is_bikini_berlin/
-http://www.25hours-hotels.com/en/bikini/home/home.html
-https://www.bikiniberlin.de/en/bikini_berlin/what_is_bikini_berlin/concept_mall_1/

GOING DUTCH

Project name_Huis ten Bosch, Sasebo-shi, Nagasaki Prefecture, Japan; Name of design firm_Nihon Sekkei Inc.; Key architects_Dr. Takekuni IKEDA; Designers_Japanese-Dutch design team; Contractor_Yoshikuni KAMICHIKA; Project completed_1992; Cost of construction_ca. 2,5-3 billion USD; Website of design firm_www. nihonsekkei.co.jp; Image sources_Figure 01_ http://upload. wikimedia.org/wikipedia/commons/8/8b/Huis_Ten_Bosch_-_01. jpg accessed 07.07.2014 (copyright: GNU Free Documentation License); Figure 02_http://upload.wikimedia.org/wikipedia/commons/5/50/Plattegrond_van_Deshima.jpg accessed 17.09.2014 (copyright: public domain); Figure 03_Ikeda, Kamichika et al.: *Huis Ten Bosch. Design Concept and its Development*. (Tokyo: Nihon Sekkei and Kodansha, 1994), 168; Figures 04 & 5_Courtesy of Iris Mach;

BIBLIOGRAPHY

-Ikeda, Takekuni, "The Spirit of the HUIS TEN BOSCH Project" in *Huis ten Bosch. Design Concept and its Development*. (Tokyo: Nihon Sekkei and Kodansha, 1994).
-A study that MIT conducted in 1997 counted 2 "gaikoku mura" among a total of 65 theme parks in Japan.
- Ikeda, Takekuni, "The Spirit of the HUIS TEN BOSCH Project" in

Huis Ten Bosch. Design Concept and its Development. (Tokyo: Nihon Sekkei and Kodansha, 1994).
-Kamichika, Yoshikuni, "*Building a Town for the Millenium*" in *Huis Ten Bosh. Design Concept and its Development.* (Tokyo: Nihon Sekkei and Kodansha, 1994).
-D'Heilly, David, "Letter from Huis Ten Bosch", *Any* 1 (4), 56-57.

MILLION DONKEY HOTEL

Project name_Million Donkey Hotel, Prata Sannita (Caserta), Italy; Name of design firm_feld 72; Key architects_Peter Zoderer; Anne Catherine Fleith, Mario Paintner, Michael Obrist, Richard Scheich; Photographer_Hertha Hurnaus; Project Completed_2005; Cost of construction_10.000 euro; Website of design firm_www.feld72.at/; Image sources_ Figure 01_ View from the inside, Million Donkey Hotel, © feld72; Figure 02_Map of the future of the Italian Small Villages. In yellow are represented the cities destined to disappear. Image courtesy of Michela Bassanelli; Figure 03_ Ruins, Valle di Zeri, Tuscany, Italy. Image courtesy of Michela Bassanelli; Figure 04_Fabrizio Favale Le Supplici, Orbita, Santarcangelo di Romagna, © Ilaria Scarpa; Figure 05_View of the bed and the garden, Million Donkey Hotel, © feld72; Figure 06_ Million Donkey Hotel, © feld72; Figure 07_ View from the outdoor bed, Million Donkey Hotel, © feld72;

BIBLIOGRAPHY

-Ashworth, Gregory J. and Brian Graham, eds. *Senses of Place: Senses of Time*. Aldershot: Ashgate, 2005.
-Carmen, Monica and Lanza, Orlando. *Urban Node: Laboratorio della Memoria*. Mantova: Corraini, 2008.
-Chambers, Iain. *Paesaggi Migratori. Cultura e identità nell'epoca postcoloniale*. Roma: Meltemi, 2003.
-Goldberg, RoseLee. *Performance Art: From Futurism to the Present*. London: Thames and Hudson, (1979) 2011.
-Graham, Brian and Howard, Peter. *The Ashgate Research Companion to Heritage and Identity*. Aldershot: Ashgate, 2008.
-Kwinter, Sanford. *Architectures of Time: Toward a Theory of the Event in Modernist Culture*. Massachusetts: MIT Press, 2002.
-Jackson, Anthony and Kidd, Jenny. *Performing Heritage: Research, Practice and Innovation in Museum Theatre and Live Interpretation*. Manchester: Manchester University Press, 2011.
-Jackson, Anthony and Rees, Leahy H. "Seeing it for real…? Authenticity, theatre and learning in museums." *Research in Drama Education* 10 (3): 303-325, 2005.
-Lacy, Suzanne. *Leaving Art. Writings on Performance, Politics and Publics, 1974-2007*. Durham: Duke University Press, 2010.
-Paesesaggio Workgroup, ed. *Villaggio dell'arte. Arte, paesaggio e produzione*. Roma: Artemide, 2008.
-Tarpino, Antonella. *Geografie della memoria. Case, rovine, oggetti quotidiani*. Milano: Einaudi, 2008.
-Teti, Vito. *Il senso dei luoghi. Memoria e storia dei paesi abbandonati*. Roma: Donzelli Editore, 2004.

A FUTURE OF PILGRIMAGE

Project name_Deus Ex Machina, Whatipu, Auckland, New Zealand; Key architect_Andy Lockyer; Project completed_2013; Website of design firm_www.halliondesign.co.nz; Image sources_Courtesy of Andy Lockyer

BIBLIOGRAPHY

-Krakauer, Jon. *Into the Wild*. New York: Anchor Books, 1997.
-*Into the Wild*. Dir. Sean Penn. Perf. Emile Hirsch, Maria Gay Harden, William Hurt, Jena Malone. Paramount Vantage, 2008.

BETWEEN MEMORY AND INVENTION

Name of design firm_Nieto Sobejano Arquitectos; Website of design firm_www.nietosobejano.com/;

Figure 01_Author: F. Català-Roca. *Eduardo Chillida en el Peine del Viento*. San Sebastián. 1976 – ©Photographic Archive F. Català-Roca – Arxiu Fotogràfic de l'Arxiu Històric del Collegi d'Architectes de Catalunya (AHCOAC). With the collaboration of the Collegi d'Architectes de Catalunya; Figure 02_Courtesy of Idoia Murga Castro and Amaya Murga Castro; Figure 03_Author unknown, http://www.guregipuzkoa.net/photo/1079928?lang=es; Figure 04-10 Name of Project_Extension of San Telmo Museum, San Seвastián, Spain; Names of artists involved with the façade project_ Leopoldo Ferrán, Agustina Otero; Names of collaborators involved with the project_Stephen Belton, Patricia Grande, Pedro Guedes, Joachim Kraft, Juan Carlos Redondo, Alexandra Sobral; Designers_Fuensanta Nieto, Enrique Sobejano; Owner_City Council San Sebastián; Structural Engineer_ N.B.35, S.L.; Plans, sections site plans, courtesy of Nieto Sobejano Arquitectos; Figures 08-09, 17 Photographer_ Courtesy of Fernando Alda Fotografia SL; Year Completed_2011;

Figures 11-13_Name of Project_Moritzburg Museum, Halle (Saale), Germany; Designers_Fuensanta Nieto, Enrique Sobejano; Owner_Stiftung Moritzburg, State – Anhalt; Structural Engineer_ GSE Ingenieur–GmbH; Photographer_Roland Halbe Architectural Photography; Section drawing_Courtesy of Nieto Sobejano Arquitectos; Year Completed_2008;

Figures 14-15_Name of Project_Center for Contemporary Art, Córdoba, Spain; Names of artist involved with the façade project_realities:united; Designers_Fuensanta Nieto, Enrique Sobejano; Owner_Junta de Andalucía (City Council); Structural Engineer_N.B.35, S.L.; Photographer_Roland Halbe Architectural Photography; Year Completed_2013;

Figures 16, 18_Name of Project_Congress Center, Mérida, Spain; Artist involved with the façade project_Esther Pizarro; Designers_ Fuensanta Nieto, Enrique Sobejano; Owner_Junta de Extremadura (City Council); Structural Engineer_N.B.35, S.L.; Photographer_Roland Halbe Architectural Photography; Year Completed_2004;

Figures 19-21_Name of Project_Joanneumsviertel, Graz, Austria; Designers_Fuensanta Nieto, Enrique Sobejano; Owner_Estiria City Council; Structural Engineer_DI. Manfred Petschnigg ZT; Photographer_Roland Halbe Architectural Photography; Section drawing: Courtesy of Nieto Sobejano Arquitectos; Year Completed_2013;

Figures 22-24_Name of Project_Castillo de la Luz, Las Palmas de Gran Canaria, Spain; Designers_Fuensanta Nieto, Enrique Sobejano; Owner_Ministry of Construction (State); Structural Engineer_N.B.35, S.L.; Photographer_Roland Halbe Architectural Photography; Year Completed_First phase, 2004 & second phase, 2013;

BIBLIOGRAPHY

_Lorentzen, Anne. "Citizens in the Experience Economy," in *European Planning Studies* Vol. 17, No. 6, Routledge, London, June 2009.
_ Chillida, Eduardo. "Escritos", *La Fábrica*, Madrid, 2005.
_ San Sebastián 2016: Proposed Application for the Title of European Capital of Culture *http://www.donostiasansebastian2016.eu/web/guest/proyecto-cultural/proyecto-final*

COLOPHON

AUTHORS

Tiziano Aglieri Rinella is an architect and assistant professor of Interior Architecture at IULM University in Milan. Aglieri Rinella holds a Ph.D. in Architecture from the Universities of Palermo and Geneva. In 2002, Aglieri Rinella was awarded the Le Corbusier Foundation scholarship. Following this award, Aglieri Rinella has concerned himself with the safeguard of Corbusier's built works. Aglieri Rinella has authored books and articles, consulted for UNESCO, and is a frequent speaker at international conferences. In addition to adaptive reuse, Aglieri Rinella's interests include new design trends within hospitality and food-related spaces. Aglieri Rinella is currently an adjunct professor of Hotel Design at the International University of Bad Honnef, Germany.

Michela Bassanelli is an Architect with a Ph.D. in Interior Architecture and Exhibition Design from the Politecnico di Milano. Bassanelli's research focuses on subjects such as: domestic interiors, "museography", collective memory, and cultural identity. Within her research, Bassanelli questions relations among cultures of dwelling, domestic architecture, and modernity. Additionally, Bassanelli investigates ways of preserving and diffusing collective memory and cultural identity. Bassanelli's current research seeks to develop an understanding of strategies for possible re-activation of abandoned hamlets as well as research on strategies to reuse crucial memories and heritage from a "museographical" point of view.

Jeffry Burchard, a practicing Architect at Machado and Silvetti Associates in Boston, has collaborated on over 25 million square feet of buildings in New York, Malaysia, Vietnam, and numerous other locations throughout the world. Burchard graduated with distinction from the Harvard Graduate School of Design as a post-professional M.Arch II student. Burchard, now a faculty member of architecture at Harvard's GSD, has reviewed student work at the Architectural Association, RISD, Columbia, MIT, the University of Toronto, Cornell, Pratt, Northeastern, UPenn and the New York Institute of Technology. Burchard's professional work centers on themes of continuity, nuance, and formal precision in architecture.

Samaa Elimam, a designer and part-time architecture studio instructor at the American University in Cairo, earned her B.A. in Architecture with Highest Honors from UC Berkeley. Elimam went on to gain a Masters of Architecture with Distinction from the Harvard Graduate School of Design. Elimam's interests include large-scale public architecture, infrastructure, and urban design projects; as well as issues related to image, perception, object agency, and preservation. Elimam has practiced architecture in Cairo, Los Angeles, and San Francisco. Elimam begins her PhD in Architectural studies at Harvard this Fall.

Eli Feldman, upon graduating from Boston University's School of Hospitality Administration, began his career in management with internships at Danny Meyer's Union Square Cafe and Gordon Ramsay's Royal Hospital Road. In 2002, Feldman began a nine-year stint at Barbara Lynch's No. 9 Park, during which he played a critical role in the company's dramatic expansion. In 2011, Feldman founded Three Princes Consulting where he worked with chefs, restauranteurs, and hospitality technology companies in Boston and New York. In 2014 Feldman co-founded Clothbound, a platform for hiring and job seeking in independent restaurants.

Laura F. Gibellini is a visual artist who holds a Ph.D. in Contemporary Art Theory from Complutense University of Madrid. In addition to her position as faculty member at the School of Visual Arts, Gibellini is currently in residency at El Museo de Los Sures, both of which are in New York City. Gibellini's most recent projects include a permanent public art installation for three subway stations commissioned by the Metropolitan Transportation Authority of New York City, and a site specific installation in Carpe Diem | Arte e Pesquisa, Lisbon. Gibellini's first book, *Construyendo un Lugar* (Constructing a Place), was published by Complutense University of Madrid in 2012.

Sylvia Leydecker, a leading interior architect in Germany, studied at the University of Applied Sciences in Wiesbaden, Germany and at the University Trisakti in Jakarta, Indonesia. Leydecker's work from her studio in Cologne ranges from creative interior concepting and design, to trendspotting. Additionally, Leydecker has a well-established expertise in healthcare and hospital design. Leydecker has authored books such as, *Corporate Interiors (2014) Nanomaterials in Architecture, InteriorArchitecture and Design* and has served as editor to leading Interior Architecture publications. Leydecker is currently the vice president of the German Association of Interior Designers and a board member at the International Federation of Interior Architects/Designers.

Andy Lockyer, currently a practicing architect at Hallion Design, was raised in New Zealand and graduated with a Masters of Architecture with First Class Honors from the University of Auckland. Lockyer's research seeks to apply the logic and mathematical principles of biological systems within the design of architectural space. Lockyer's work at Hallion Design, a boutique multinational office specializing in commercial architecture, explores the intersection of human and environmental systems in projects ranging from objects to masterplans. Lockyer is currently focusing on how to apply his research to the development of architecture and spaces that are sympathetic to the human condition.

Iris Mach, Senior Scientist at the Vienna University of Technology, researches and teaches architecture in the fields of "Disaster Mitigation" and "Applied Aesthetics". Additionally, Mach heads the scientific cooperation program between the Vienna University of Technology and select Japanese universities. Mach graduated from the Vienna University of Technology and began research as a postgraduate student at the University of Tokyo. Her doctoral studies began in Tokyo with a focus on staged spaces in traditional and modern Japanese architecture and were completed upon her return to the Vienna University of Technology.

Dionys Ottl worked for RRP Architekten from 1989 to 1992 with a focus on hospital design and other sectors of social architecture. In 1992 Ottl began work as an assistant in the KPS studio and then in 1994 for Hild and Kaltwasser Architekten. Following this, Ottl created the Munich based studio Hild und K Architekten along with Andreas Hild. In addition to his studio work, Ottl is a published author, lecturer, and a critic in Germany and Canada. Ottl holds a degree from the Technische Universität München.

Ann Petermans holds a Ph.D. in Architecture from Hasselt University in Belgium where she is currently a Postdoctoral Researcher. Petermans' primary research interests include design for subjective wellbeing and happiness as well as designing for experience within architectural and interior environments for diverse user groups. Petermans has presented her work at various international conferences and has been published in multiple periodicals such as the *International Journal of Design* and the *Journal of Interior Design*. In addition to her research, Petermans teaches a course on design for subjective wellbeing and happiness in the Bachelor's and Master's Departments of Architecture and Interior Architecture respectively, at Hasselt University.

Bie Plevoets studied Interior Architecture at the PHL University College in Belgium. Plevoets holds a Masters in Conservation of Monuments and Sites from the Raymond Lemaire International Centre for Conservation, as well as a Ph.D. in Architecture from Hasselt University. Plevoets' doctoral work explored the role of adaptive reuse within interior architecture specifically focusing on retail as a new function. Plevoets' postdoctoral work at Hasselt University includes a continued investigation of this emerging theory within adaptive reuse interior architecture, as well as teaching several courses on adaptive reuse in the Bachelor and Masters programs within the Interior Architecture Department.

Patrick Ruggiero, Jr., a designer at Machado Silvetti Associates in Boston, earned his BArch with distinction from Syracuse University in 2013. Originally from Bethlehem, Pennsylvania, Ruggiero has worked with Rick Joy Architects, Spillman Farmer Architects, and EFGH. From examining the relationship between the built environment and economic and political systems, to engaging digital media through an architectural lens, Ruggiero's work explores a range of topics. In total, Ruggiero's work seeks to use architecture as a means of creating civic, commercial, and social value to both clients and a broader architectural discourse.

Luis Sacristán Murga received his architectural education from several universities including the Polytechnic School of Madrid in Spain, Lunds Tekniska Högskola in Sweden, and the Rhode Island School of Design, in the USA. Sacristán Murga, currently a practicing architect in London, has worked as an architect in Denmark and the USA. As well as organizing architectural workshops in London, Sacristán Murga serves as a guest critic at the Architectural Association. Through the principles of adaptive reuse and the use of public space, Sacristán Murga works to understand the ways in which architecture can transform consciousness and merge with nature.

Koenraad Van Cleempoel has been engaged in establishing and directing a research unit focused on interior architecture at Hasselt University since 2005. At Hasselt, Van Cleempoel supervises several Ph.D. students' work regarding aspects of adaptive reuse in interior architecture. Van Cleempoel has a particular interest in the theoretical discourse surrounding the reuse of heritage buildings, which he believes to be linked to the emergence of interior architecture as a formal academic discipline. Van Cleempoel has studied in Louvain and Madrid and holds a Ph.D. in Art History from the Warburg Institute in London.

EDITORS

Ernesto Aparicio is a Senior Critic in the Graphic Design Department at RISD. He earned his BA at the Escuela de Bellas Artes, La Plata, Buenos Aires and his Post Graduate Studies at the Ecole des Art Decoratifs, Paris. Prior to moving to the US he served as Art Director for Editions du Seuil in Paris, while maintaining his own Graphic Design practice, Aparicio Design Inc. Best known for his work in the world of publishing, his work has also included corporate identities, publications and way-finding for corporations and institutions in France, Japan, and the US. He has recently been named Creative Director for the New York design firm, DFA.

Markus Berger is Associate Professor and Graduate Program Director in the Department of Interior Architecture at RISD. He holds a Diplomingenieur für Architektur from the Technische Universität Wien, Austria and is a registered architect (SBA) in the Netherlands. Prior to coming to the USA, Berger practiced as an architect with UN Studios and taught in Austria, India, and Pakistan. Berger currently heads his own design studio in Providence, InsideOut Interventions, focusing on design interventions and research such as forms of *CHANGE* in the built environment and *UMBAU*, design interventions that take sensory experience as an essential part of the whole. Berger is a co-founder and co-editor of the Int|AR Journal.

Jeffrey Katz has a Bachelor of Architecture from Carnegie Mellon University and a Master of Architecture from the Graduate School of Design at Harvard University. Upon completing his graduate degree, Katz joined the faculty of the Architecture Department at RISD. Katz and his wife, Cheryl, started C&J Katz Studio in 1984. The studio's work includes retail, workspace, residential, exhibition, and furniture design. As his practice evolved, Jeffrey transitioned to the Interior Architecture Department where he is currently a Senior Critic. The focus of his design studios at RISD has been retail and hospitality design.

Liliane Wong is Professor and Head of the Department of Interior Architecture at RISD. She received her Master of Architecture from Harvard University, Graduate School of Design and a Bachelor of Art in Mathematics from Vassar College. She is a registered Architect in Massachusetts and has practiced in the Boston area including in her firm, MWA where she focused on the design of libraries. She is a co-designer of the library furniture system, Kore. A long time volunteer at soup kitchens, her teaching emphasizes the importance of public engagement in architecture and design. She is a co-founder and co-editor of the Int|AR Journal.

Int|AR

Department of Interior Architecture
Rhode Island School of Design

SINCE 2010

MDES Interior Studies
[Adaptive Reuse]

The existing 2+ year Master of Design (MDes) in Interior Studies [Adaptive Reuse] provides a unique design education on the alteration of existing structures through interior interventions and adaptive reuse. The program establishes a clear aesthetic, theoretical and technological framework for the study of interior studies and adaptive reuse. Graduating students are properly equipped to engage in this subject in the general design field and to develop strategies in their work which recognize the importance of social and environmental responsibility.

NEW TRACK, STARTING 2016

MDES Interior Studies
[Exhibition & Narrative Environments]

The study of Exhibition and Narrative Environments has been a part of our departmental studio offerings for many years. Our department has hosted annual studios specific to the design of the narrative environment that featured collaborations with the key members of the RISD Museum, the RISD Departments of Graphic Design, History of Art & Visual Culture and Brown University, in particular, the Haffenreffer Museum and the John Nicholas Brown Center. The new track on Exhibition and Narrative Environments consists of an MDes curriculum supported by courses offered in these other disciplines, formalizing the existing relationships with these departments.

SINCE 2010

MA Adaptive Reuse

Formerly called "MA Interior Architecture [ADAPTIVE REUSE]", the purpose of the Master of Arts (MA) in Adaptive Reuse is to provide a unique specialist design education on the subject of adaptive reuse as a post-professional study to a first degree in Architecture. The program aims to establish a clear aesthetic, theoretical and technological framework for the study of adaptive reuse, in order that graduating students are properly equipped to engage in the practice of working with existing buildings, structures and spaces. It enables students to develop strategies in their work which recognize the importance of social and environmental responsibility.

SINCE 2010

BFA Interior Studies
[Adaptive Reuse]

The BFA is centered on rethinking the life of existing spaces – through design alterations, renovations and adaptive reuse, but encompasses also a very wide range of studies that engage with existing fabric, from installation design and retail design to more traditional interior design.